PARADISE IN
LIFE IN THE GRE
1929-1939

By
Jack L. McSherry, Jr.

PARADISE IN SUNNYSIDE
LIFE IN THE GREAT DEPRESSION

PARADISE IN SUNNYSIDE
LIFE IN THE GREAT DEPRESSION

The Village of Sunnyside in 1930

INTRODUCTION

Jack L. McSherry was discharged from the United States Navy in the year 1923 after having served for sixteen years, which included the cruise around the world, of 1907-1909, with Theodore Roosevelt's Great White Fleet of sixteen battleships. He also served in World War I. At the time, McSherry's father lived in Lancaster, Pennsylvania, so McSherry took up residence with his father until such time as he could reestablish himself into civilian life. His Mother had died when he was thirteen years old and was living on a farm near Airville, PA in York County.

Before long, McSherry read an article in the newspaper concerning a Harrisburg Engineering firm which was going to build a dam for the Roaring Creek Water Company in Bear Gap, Pennsylvania. McSherry's Father was a carpenter, so McSherry gathered up some basic tools and headed for Bear Gap. He was immediately hired by

Gannett, Eastman, Fleming, who were not only the Engineers for the job, but also the Contractor. He first went to work on an existing dam, known as #6 dam, several miles upstream from the dam that they were planning to build, where they were repairing, improving, and enlarging the existing dam. After working on the upper dam for a while, he finally was sent to the site of the proposed new dam, known as #2 dam, where he worked on whatever they wanted him to do.

While working on the construction of # 2 dam, he became friends with Calvin Burrell, who was another workman on the construction of #2 dam. They became very good friends, and eventually, Calvin invited McSherry to come to his house after work for dinner. Calvin's home was a very short distance from the worksite. Calvin's father worked for the Roaring Creek Water Company as the Engineer for the operation of the water pump station which was located very close to #2 dam, and he and his family lived in a house situated on water company property.

McSherry went to the Burrell home where he met the members of Calvin's family. Calvin was unmarried, as were his two brothers, Bertlette and David, but they all three lived with their parents, David and Cora Burrell. Calvin had a sister, Ivy, living there also. Ivy was engaged to a gentleman who lived in the nearby Village of Elysburg. However, after many visits to her family by Calvin's friend, Jack McSherry, she was apparently overwhelmed by the conversations about people, places and things all over the world, and the good manners of Calvin's handsome friend. Mr. McSherry was a man who knew no prejudices, a man without vindictiveness, and a man without enemy. She broke her engagement to the gentleman in Elysburg. Jack McSherry and Ivy Burrell were married in March 1925.

They remained living in the Burrell home for some time after they were married. While living there they had two sons, William and David. In 1927, they purchased a house in the Village of Sunnyside, which was about five miles from the Burrell home. In the year 1928, while the family lived in Sunnyside, Jack, Jr. was born in the office of Dr. W. J. Harris located at 11 N. Market Street in Shamokin.

In the year 1929, the sky fell, gloom befell the nation, the great depression created chaos with bankruptcy, unemployment, hunger, agony and fear.

To the McSherry children, being only a little over a year old to four years old, in the Village of Sunnyside, Ralpho Township, Northumberland County, Pennsylvania, there was none of the above. The three kids lived, safely, in a house with their parents. The kids were caressed, were never hungry, and enjoyed every day. Friends came regularly to the McSherry house to play. The McSherry family was not rich, but was not poor. Mr. McSherry, having served in the Navy for sixteen years, was now in the Fleet Reserve. This created a small, steady income which supplemented his earnings as he worked at the Eagle Silk Mill in Shamokin.

As the time moved on, Mr. McSherry was laid off at the silk mill because of the depression. However, his Fleet Reserve income was still coming. He worked wherever he could to enhance his income. On occasion, he worked as a laborer for the local water company, he was hired by a neighbor to build a garage. He apparently constructed the garage very well because it is still standing today. He helped build a house in the neighborhood for a local landowner. By doing this, he was able to feed and house his family adequately. In addition to providing for his family, he quietly delivered food and other assistance to neighbors who were not faring as well. That was the nature of family life in the Great Depression.

However, the children of the neighborhood never seemed to know that there was a problem. They were happy, played, and enjoyed their childhood. Yes, in colder weather, some of the children did not have warm jackets, but they found other ways to keep warm, possibly by wearing several shirts and a sweater. It was the common thing for the boys to wear overalls most of the time. The knees would wear out in the overalls and the Mothers would sew on patches. This was worn everywhere, even to school and was totally acceptable because everyone did it. The people made the best of their situation and showed happiness at all times. Without a doubt, all parents at that time had major concerns. They had to take care of their family, feed them, and look out for them, but the children lived in Paradise.

Dad holding Jack, Jr.
1928

Bill & Beah
1929

This document was not based on research of news items, or governmental workings, or histories of the Depression, but only through the eyes of a child who lived through the Great Depression

CHAPTER 1
SUNNYSIDE

In 1927, Jack & Ivy McSherry purchased a house in the new subdivision, entitled Sunnyside, which was located in Ralpho Township, Northumberland County, Pennsylvania, approximately three miles north of the Borough of Shamokin. The new house was half of a double house. Along with the lot on which the house was located, they also purchased two additional lots adjacent to the house. The result was that they had a house with a very big yard.

The McSherry Home
1931

The new house had a living room, dining room and kitchen on the first floor. On the second floor were three bedrooms, a large closet, and a completely modern bathroom, with a flush toilet, and a bathtub with four ball and claw legs. The house had a full-size basement. In the rear was a closed in porch, and in the front, a large, under roof, porch.

The three boys slept in the same bedroom. Bill and Dave slept in a double bed, and Jack slept in a crib from his baby days until he was six years old. He had no objection to that, it was a large crib. Above Jack's crib, hanging on the wall, was a picture of a dog howling in a snowstorm to let his owners know that he had found the lost sheep. Jack came home from school one day and found a new, single bed in the bedroom, and the crib was gone. Jack was happy with his new bed.

The McSherry house was heated by a central heating system, which consisted of a large, coal-burning furnace in the basement. Directly above the furnace was a 30" square grating in the floor which allowed the warm air to come into the living room/dining room area. That was the extent of the distribution of the heat. The heat traveled throughout the house as the required doors were opened.

Shortly after purchasing the house, the McSherrys acquired an electric refrigerator. The refrigerator was located in a corner of the dining room. Directly below the refrigerator, in the basement, was a large compressor which was connected to an electric motor with a belt. This compressor would automatically start and stop as required. The refrigerator was a rarity. Almost everyone else had an ice box.

In 1936, the McSherrys abandoned their coal stove in the kitchen and installed a new electric stove. This was also a rarity in the neighborhood. With the coal stove on a hot summer day, it was rather warm sitting at the kitchen table for dinner within two feet of the coal stove.

To clean the carpets, Mrs. McSherry had an electric sweeper, which was not common in the area.   She also had a Maytag washing machine, complete with a wringer. The laundry soap, super suds, was a powder which came in a box. Super Suds made the first singing commercial for radio broadcast.   "Super Suds, Super Suds, wash your duds with Super suds". Dad built a clothes line in the back yard for her to hang the clothes to dry.

Electrical power was provided to Sunnyside, and most of the nearby areas, by the Pennsylvania Power and light Company

Jack   1928

During the entire depression, the McSherrys had a telephone. It was a party line, meaning that more than one family was connected to that phone line. The line that the McSherrys were on had only two families on it. If the phone rang with one ring, it was for the McSherrys. If the phone rang with two rings, it was for the other party. If the one party was on the phone, the other person could listen in to their conversation if they chose to do so. To use the phone, the phone was picked up and held to the ear. The operator would say "number please", then the desired phone number would be told to the operator and she would make the connection. The McSherry's phone number was 941-R-1.

The McSherrys had a neighbor lady who did not have a telephone. At least twice a day, she would knock on the door and ask to use the telephone. Mrs. McSherry always allowed her to do so. The neighbor lady always called the same number, 773-J-3. That was the number of another lady who lived in Overlook. The conversations were never anything of importance, just talk. Another consequence to these frequent trips to the telephone was that the McSherry's carpet in the living room was worn threadbare in a path directly from the front door to the telephone.

Prince Albert tobacco for pipes and cigarettes was sold in a can. The kids thought it was funny to call the local stores on the phone and ask them if they had Prince Albert in a can. If the answer was "yes", they then retorted, "well let him out". OK, so it's not too funny!

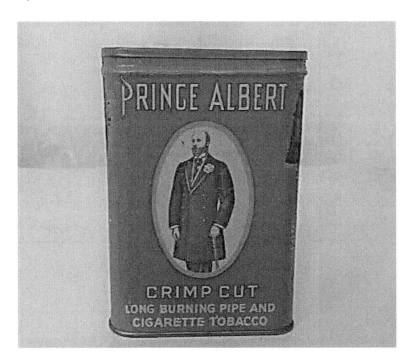

Prince Albert in a can

SHAMOKIN

AND NEARBY POINTS

TELEPHONE DIRECTORY

FEBRUARY - 1939

THE BELL TELEPHONE COMPANY OF PENNSYLVANIA

SEE PAGES 1 TO 6 FOR EMERGENCY CALLS AND OTHER IMPORTANT INFORMATION

"WHERE TO BUY IT"—*See Yellow Pages*

12

Sunnyside consisted of several streets, and about twenty homes. The streets were unpaved, including the main road running adjacent to Sunnyside, which ran from the village of Weigh Scales to Bear Gap. The oldest house in the subdivision existed many years prior to the development of Sunnyside and was at one time a tavern and stage coach stop. The house was located about 300 feet in front and to the right of the McSherry home, and was occupied by the Chaundy family. The barn, which served as a livery stable for the tavern, was behind the Chaundy house and directly in front of the McSherry residence. During the time that the McSherry family lived there, the barn was used only for storage. The barn was torn down around the year 1938.

The kids often found Indian head pennies in the area around the barn. Apparently they were lost by someone back in the days when the barn was still a livery stable.

Indian Head Pennies

Sunnyside had a south and west exposure to the sun, therefore, the name was appropriate. The front of the McSherry house faced the south. Behind the house was a farm. To the east there were open fields and behind the fields were woods extending into a mountain which existed between Sunnyside and Shamokin. The westerly sun lit up the green fields and the green mountainside to the east. The McSherry house was slightly set aside from the remainder of the Village. The primary portion of Sunnyside was located in front, and to the south, of the McSherry home. To the west of the McSherry home were several houses, the road from Weigh Scales to Bear Gap, and beyond that, the Pennsylvania Railroad. Still further away, but in view was another mountain. On the side of that mountain was the Reading Railroad. Adjacent to the mountain, and beyond the Reading Railroad, was a lower elevation consisting of grasslands. It was in that location that prevailing oncoming storms could be observed.

Bill, Jack & Dave
1930

Mom & Jack
1930

Dad
1930

Bill 1930

Dave 1930

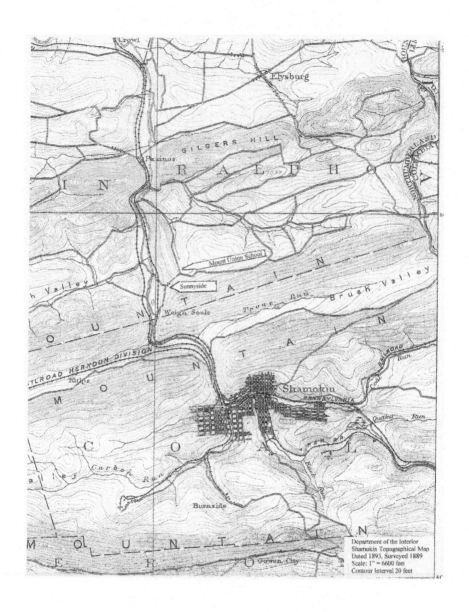

,

18

The McSherry Family
1933

Sunnyside, and the lands around it, was primarily an agricultural area. The coal mining areas were separated from Sunnyside by a mountain. The Sunnyside side of the mountain was natural, full of trees, and beautiful to look at. The other side contained coal mine waste. The basic coal mining was with the large colleries, however the area was peppered with independent coal mines, quite often not approved by the land owner. These miners were called bootleggers. Subsidiary coal mining operations included independent coal breakers. These coal breaker establishments would buy unprocessed, bulk coal from the miners. They then crushed it, separated it into different sizes, washed it and sold it. There were many of these breakers in the coal mining areas.

Sunnyside was a unique place to live. Even though the fields and woods on the adjacent land were privately owned, the owners had no objection to people walking on their land at any time. As a result, the McSherry children had free access and use of the land as though it were their own property. Not only did they walk on and through the property on a regular basis, they also constructed huts on it, picked berries, climbed trees, hiked to the top of the mountain, and freely used the land for their childhood pleasures without hesitation.

In the woods and fields in and around Sunnyside, there were black snakes, garter snakes and green snakes, but no copperheads or rattle snakes. There were also rabbits and some other small animals, but there were no deer. There were also many box turtles. The snakes that were there were harmless, however, they scared some people just because they were snakes.

In the area of Sunnyside, there were springs, some just ponding, then flowing away. Others consisted of small pipes protruding from the ground with a continuous flow of water. The kids knew where all of these water sources existed, and drank from them regularly and freely. Was the water from these pipes pure? No one ever worried about that, or even thought of it. As far as is known, no one ever got sick from drinking the water.

The water for the McSherry family, as well as several other houses in their vicinity, came from a shallow underground source located nearby. On this water source was a windmill which operated a pump. The pump sent the water up on the hill, several hundred feet to the east of the McSherry house, to an underground reservoir. The water flowed from the reservoir in pipes, by gravity, to the houses. The pressure was very low, but it sufficed. It was probably around 1938 when this system was abandoned when a piping system was installed by the Roaring Creek Water Company.

Margaret Mauser

One day, Dave and Jack were heading for home from the mountainside, where they were busy doing something, and as they walked past the reservoir, they heard whimpering and crying of little kids. It seemed to come from the reservoir. They went over to the reservoir, which was no longer in use, and looked into a square opening in the top slab of the reservoir. To their surprise, at the bottom of the reservoir they saw two little kids standing and crying in about a foot of water. Apparently they were walking on the top of the reservoir and it collapsed dropping them into the water. Fortunately they were ok, just scared. Dave and Jack didn't particularly know how to get them out of the reservoir, so they ran down the hill to the McSherry house and told their mother that Margaret Mauser and Franklin Roosevelt Chaundy were in the reservoir. Mom thought the worst and ran outside and called to Margaret's father who happened to be outside of his house at the time. Mr. Mauser immediately ran full speed up the hill to the reservoir and lifted the scared kids out of the reservoir. Both kids were ok, just a little upset. Fortunately the reservoir was no longer in use, and the 12" of water cushioned their fall. The reservoir was at least six feet deep.

The McSherry house had a proper sewerage system. The sewage was piped into a cesspool located in the lawn at the front of the house. A cesspool consists of a hole, about four feet square and six feet deep lined with rocks. The sewage entered the cesspool and seeped into the soil at its bottom. This cesspool would have been constructed when the house was built, which was in the years 1926-1927. Around 1934 or 1935, Jack was in the front yard playing with the neighbor's dog, Skippy, when the ground opened up and Skippy fell in. The cesspool had become oversaturated and the surface collapsed. Skippy was immediately rescued by Mr. McSherry. Therefore, the cesspool had a working lifetime of about eight years.

Within a day or so, Mr. McSherry dug a new cesspool hole a short distance from the failed one. He did not put in the rock, or do the piping yet because he had to be on his job. Little Jack showed interest in the hole, and to further investigate it, he jumped into it. After a very short time in the hole, Jack realized that he was unable to climb back out of this very deep hole. Probably after some hardy screaming his Mother came out and pulled him out of the hole. Days later, the new cesspool was put into service.

Most of the people who lived in the rural areas did not have indoor bathrooms. They had outhouses in their back yard. Jack's grandparents had an outhouse. Going to that outhouse on a cold winter day was quite an experience, especially when the wind was blowing through the cracks in the outhouse wall. The toilet paper in the outhouse was usually a Montgomery Ward's catalog.

The Outhouse

Public sewer systems did not exist in Shamokin or in any of the surrounding areas. Sewage in Shamokin was accumulated in pipes in some areas which conveyed the sewage to, and discharged it into, the Shamokin Creek, which ran through the Borough. Individual houses located near the creek piped their sewage directly into the creek. Eventually, all the sewage from

Shamokin found its way into the Shamokin Creek. The downstream communities and homes did the same. The water in the Shamokin Creek was black because it also received all the wastewater from the mines and the coal washeries. Whenever the mines closed down, usually because of an employee strike, the Creek would not run black, it become a brownish yellow. When the water was brownish yellow, it let off a foul odor. The people were happy when the miners went back to work because the water would again flow black and the foul odors discontinued. Apparently the coal runoff countered the bad odors of the sewage.

Fortunately, the closest that the Shamokin creek came to Sunnyside was where it flowed through the Village of Weigh Scales which is about a mile from Sunnyside. Sunnyside never smelled the odors from the creek.

The Village of Weigh Scales is mentioned periodically throughout this presentation. Since the name is unusual, it has been determined that the name should be explained. Following is a photograph of a portion of the Village of Weigh Scales. Weigh Scales consisted of the buildings as shown on the photograph which, were the primary buildings, including the Hotel. In addition to the Hotel, there were houses situated on that same side of the highway extending behind the photographers location for about a quarter mile along the highway. At the end of the row of houses was Hoover's gas station. Directly across the highway from the hotel, and shown on the photograph, is a building that was a scale house for the railroad. On the other side of the scale house were the tracks for the Pennsylvania Railroad. Trains were made up at this location where the various cars were weighed, then drifted down the tracks where they were sent by a switchman to the proper track for their final destination. Mr. Clarence Morris of Overlook was the weighmaster who performed the operations of the scale house. Mr. Morris walked to and from Weigh Scales every day to work, a distance of one mile each way.

Since there existed a scale house in that location, the Village was named Weigh Scales.

The Village of Weigh Scales

When the McSherry children were very young, Mrs. McSherry's niece, Eleanor Fertig, would stay with the McSherry Family all summer. She did this regularly for several years. Eleanor was a teenager at the time. She enjoyed being there and the McSherry kids liked her very much. One of Eleanor's favorite outings for the kids was to hike across the fields of the Elwood Bailey farm, past the Mount Union School in Overlook to the George Bailey farm. There was a small woods with a creek flowing through it on the George Bailey farm. This area was also a pasture for Mr. Bailey's cows. When walking in the area, the barefooted kids had to look out for the cow flops. Some of them were old and dried out so the kids could step on them, others were new and quite squishy. They had to be avoided. The banks of the small stream consisted of pure, yellow clay. This clay had the right water content to be easily molded into any shape. All kinds of statuary was shaped. The kids also made marbles with the clay. In addition to playing in the creek, the kids also played on the banks alongside the creek. They built twig huts then made twig people with acorns for the heads and placed them around the huts. Moss was used for the lawns. What fun!

While the kids were having their fun, Eleanor spent the time, close by, but visiting with George Bailey's son, Jack. They got along well, and, of course, that was probably why she took the kids there so often. Shortly after the attack on Pearl Harbor and the beginning of World War II, Eleanor, who was a registered nurse, enlisted in the United States Army, a nurse and a second lieutenant. She spent the entire war in the Army.

Jack Bailey was drafted into the Army early in the war and was sent to battle in Europe. Near the end of the war, he was badly wounded, but he survived. He returned to the Bailey farm when he was discharged from the Army. Jack and Eleanor were married and spent their lives together.

There were many children in Sunnyside. All of them attended the same school, Mount Union School, located about a half mile to the northeast in the village of Overlook. As a result, there were many friendships among them. The closest friends of the McSherry children were Harry Harper and Wayne Knoebel who lived in Sunnyside, Jack Llewellyn, Marlin Snyder and John Cook who lived in Weigh Scales, and Donald Spayd who lived in

Overlook. Although these were the closest friends, there were many others that were part of the general group of friends.

For entertainment, these young people would gather and play games, ride bikes, or play with toys, depending on their age and whatever came to mind for them to do. There was no difficulty to organize a baseball game, it was only necessary to walk outside to some common area while carrying a baseball glove. Someone would notice and would come out ready to play. More will gather and the game is on. Wayne Knoebel was a close friend and spent much time with young Jack, who was close to the same age as Wayne. In their earlier years they played with toy cars and trucks. As they got older, they played baseball, nips and other games. The kids were always outside and together.

In their younger years, Jack, Jr. and Wayne Knoebel would play with their toy cars and trucks in the unpaved driveway alongside the house. With the loose stones on the soil, it was easy for them to shape roads on the surface of the driveway with the side of the palms of their hands. These roads covered the entire area of the driveway alongside the house. In the summer, in the afternoon, the sun moved to the opposite side of the house providing shade to the play area making it a nice place to play. When the kids were playing with their toy cars in the driveway, Mom referred to that activity as "playing in the dirt".

Playing in the dirt

On the picture of the kids playing in the dirt, the side of the house is shown. This side of the house was very unique. There were lath nailed to the side of the house, then it was plastered with a stucco mix. When the stucco was still soft, small pieces of multi-colored glass were randomly cast into, and embedded into the plaster. It was unusual, but attractive.

Toy truck

Toy car

Toy tractor

Toy truck

On occasion a big thunderstorm would hit Sunnyside. The McSherry kids and their Mom would sit on the swing on the front porch and watch the storm. When the wind blew the rain onto the porch, they would go inside and watch the storm through the front window. During one of the storms, there was much lightning flashing in the sky with some of it striking objects on the ground. The kids saw the lightning strike the top of an electric pole, shooting off many flashes of blue light. Another streak of lightning flashed out of the sky and struck the roof of a house about a quarter mile away. The roof immediately erupted into flames. The volunteer firemen arrived almost instantly and put the fire out. There was some damage to the roof, but the house was saved.

After a storm, the kids would take their shoes off, if they had them on, go outside and run through the muddy pools of water.

Early in the 1930's, they paved the main road through Sunnyside with tar and stones, and rolled it with a large steam roller. While this work was going on, Wayne Knoebel and Jack sat along the road, in front of the Knoebel home, and watched. They especially enjoyed watching the big roller in action. The Knoebels had several apple trees in the back yard, and there were many half rotted apples under the trees. So Wayne and jack gathered these apples and took them out to the front of the house where they were watching the work. As the roller approached, they rolled the apples out in front of it and watched them being squashed into the pavement. That went on until they ran out of apples, and no one objected.

Wayne Knoebel's father, Herbert Knoebel was Sunnyside's barber. He had his barber shop in the basement of his house. Dad would take all three kids to the shop as necessary for a haircut. Sometimes it was a long wait if others were also there, but the conversation never stopped. The price of a haircut was thirty-five cents.

Dad made a golf course in the back yard. He made the holes by digging out the dirt several inches deep, then he inserted a tuna fish can, with no lid, into the hole, and compressed the soil against the can to keep it firmly in place and level with the surface of the ground. He placed about six or eight of these holes in various locations around the yard. To identify each hole, he nailed a number to the side of a two-inch wide stake which he pounded into the ground. The source of the numbers was from old license plates. Having finished the course, he bought some golf clubs, not professional ones, but simple clubs shaped like a putter. Each person used one of these clubs when playing the game.

The back yard also contained a swing for the kids. Dad made the swing. He hung the swing from a tree which had a large horizontal limb at the right height. He hung a wooden plank from the limb using two chains. To protect the limb from damage, he wrapped several layers of cloth around the limb before he attached the chains. This was a good swing and it provided much entertainment. Some people hung a tire from the limb of a tree to make a swing, but they were not as comfortable to sit in as the swing that Dad made.

Dad used to burn trash in a barren location about 200 feet from the house. Burning trash was a common thing during the depression. One day, Jack went to the trash burning site, and, since there was no fire at the time, he walked into the ashes and started kicking things around. Before long, he noticed that the bottom of his overalls leg was on fire. The flame was leaping upward on his right leg. Panicking, Jack ran from the fire site toward the house with flames on his pant-leg. He ran into the house and found his mother in the kitchen. Mom beat the fire out with her hands. His pants were not too badly damaged by the fire, so with the fire out, Jack went back outside to continue his self-entertainment and Mom finished her work in the kitchen.

Mr. Jack L. McSherry
(Dad)
1936

Dick Wynn, David McSherry, Harry Harper, Jack McSherry, Bill
McSherry, Wayne Knoebel
1937

If you look closely at this photo, you will see that Jack is sticking his tongue out and Bill is scolding him for doing it. Jack wore on Bill's nerves.

The depression may have been difficult for the adults, but it was paradise for the children. But, even with their worries, the adults showed a happy face. The parents had no reason to fear for the safety of their children. There was no crime, no stealing, or any other noticeable danger to the children. Toys could be left laying outside and were never stolen. A bicycle could be ridden to any location, leaned against a building or a tree, and left there while doing other things, or going away for a while, and was always there when the owner returned. At school, money, or other personal property could be placed on, or in, the desk and would never be taken by anyone. People were poor as a result of the Great Depression, but they were trustworthy and honest. Ivy McSherry very seldom knew where her children were during the day, but she had no fear that they would return safely for dinner.

In the early days, Mr. McSherry worked the night shift in the silk mill. Therefore, he slept during the days. Mrs. McSherry did her best to maintain quiet so as not to disturb his sleep. One day young Jack was throwing a rubber ball against the side of the house and then catching it as it bounced back. This made a continuous thump inside the house and especially in Mr. McSherry's bedroom. Mrs. McSherry immediately went outside to stop the source of the noise.

The average worker, during the depression, earned about twenty dollars a week.

Coins and currency from the Great Depression era

The kids had a way of earning money which required some work on their part. They would gather iron and steel, aluminum, foil paper, tires, car batteries, and similar items. Once a week, there was a truck that would go through the neighborhood ringing a bell, with the name Harrison on the side of it. This was the collector and buyer of the junk. The kids innocently called him the "Sheeny" not knowing that was a rather rude name to call him. They would have the Sheeny drive his truck to their stockpile of junk to sell it to him. The Sheeny would tell the kids how much he would give them for their junk, and it was a take it or leave it price, so the kids always accepted his offer. The going rate for tires was one cent per tire. A car battery brought five dollars, but the kids found very few of these. A small pile of iron may go for fifty cents. After doing business with Harrison for several years, a newcomer in the business started making the rounds, ringing his bell. His name was Julius Savlov. The kids liked him more than Harrison because he was a friendlier person and paid better prices.

Private enterprise prevailed during the depression without any governmental interference. A good example is that several of the older boys, possibly 12 years old, made wheelbarrows out of wood. The material to build them probably came from the dump. With these wheelbarrows they would solicit the people of Sunnyside to hire them to haul their garbage and trash to the dump for a charge of fifty cents. They did not haul the trash to the big dump where the kids got their building supplies because it was much farther away, but to an area on an unpaved road which went from Sunnyside, around a sharp curve, and across the tracks of the Pennsylvania Railroad to the main highway. There was a steep bank alongside the road with the Pennsylvania Railroad tracks below. That is where they dumped the trash and garbage. This dump was described as being down around the bend.

Speaking of the dump at down around the bend, at one time during the depression, young Jack was walking along that road and as he passed the dump on the side of the road, over the bank, he saw a man lying in the dump, trying not to be seen. The poor man was a transient, commonly called a bum, and he was scrounging through the garbage trying to find some food. The man apparently arrived on a train, and jumped off at that location. His mission of travel was to try to find work.

Airplanes during the depression would rarely be seen. If one should be seen flying over the area, everyone would be notified, and all would run outside to see it. On occasion, two planes would fly over together and that was even more exciting. Planes at that time were called aeroplanes. Occasionally a small plane would do stunts in the air such as tailspins, rolls, loops and dives. Everyone watched this with great excitement.

Jack's first airplane ride was in 1933 at the Bloomsburg fair. Dad and Bill first took a ride in a small plane, and after they landed, Jack and Dave got into the plane and took a ride.

In the late 1930's, the WPA was improving the road which ran from the entry road toward the McSherry house. WPA is the abbreviation for the Works Progress Administration, a governmental organization that provided work for people during the great depression. Even though the WPA was a governmental organization, it functioned well to provide work, and therefore, income for many men. These men worked hard and appreciated the opportunity to work. They excavated for roads, all day in the hot sun, with picks, shovels, and wheelbarrows. People in the great depression did not want a handout, and they were too proud to receive relief without working. The foreman for this project was an acquaintance of the McSherrys. We will call him Charlie. One day Charlie apparently needed a hatchet, so he walked over to the McSherry house and asked if he could borrow a hatchet. Since young Jack owned his own hatchet, he was proud and happy to loan it to Charlie. At a later time, the hatchet was properly returned to Jack. Many years later, when Jack was an adult, he was visiting Charlie at his home when Charlie showed him a stack of cancelled checks. These checks served as receipts that Charlie had properly paid the bribes, on a monthly basis, in order to get the job as a Foreman. Charlie was very proud that he was able to pay the bribes as necessary. Hopefully the entire WPA system was not so contaminated.

At one point in the project, as the work was underway, they used a large steam-driven roller to compact the soils on the road. In the evening, they parked the roller alongside the road across the street from the Ralph Cook family's home. However, since it was a steam roller, upon parking the machine, there was still heat in the fire chamber and steam pressure in the system. Bill, Dave, Jack, John Cook, and several others went to the roller. Most climbed onto the operator's platform to take a good look. Bill was the first on and stood adjacent to the control equipment. He pushed a large lever forward which resulted in a large flywheel to start spinning, and the roller started to chug forward. All of the kids jumped off of the roller, as it was moving forward, and ran toward the McSherry home. Apparently Mr. Cook noticed the roller moving, ran out of his house, and stopped it. Nothing more was ever heard about that incident.

On the road building project in Sunnyside, the WPA also had a dump truck which transported excess dirt from place to place. This dump truck was about the size of a large pickup truck, but it had the mechanism to dump the load. However, whenever the truck was working, there was a continuous flow of steam coming out of the radiator.

It was not uncommon, as the WPA truck went by with the men standing in the box of the truck holding their tools, on the way to their work, that people, and sometimes kids, would shout at them "we poke along", a secondary name for the initials WPA. Most people frowned on this because they respected the workmen and did not like to see them insulted in this manner.

When Mr. McSherry was laid off from the Eagle Silk Mill because of the depression, he found other ways to earn money to support his family. His father was a carpenter, so he felt that he was capable as a carpenter also. He was hired by the neighbor to build a garage. He built the garage. At that time, contractors were not licensed by the State, and there were no building permits to acquire. That was known as free enterprise. He extended his carpenter work by assisting to build a house for a nearby neighbor.

The basement for the house was excavated by a horse-drawn scoop. As the scoop approached the soil to be excavated, the operator lifted the handles of the scoop so that it cut into the soil thereby self-loading itself. The horse then pulled the scoop to the opposite end of the proposed house where the operator of the scoop lifted the handles and dumped the load. They then circled the house and went through the same procedure for the remaining areas to be excavated

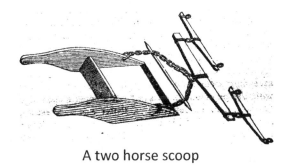

A two horse scoop

They formed the basement walls and were pouring the concrete. The concrete was mixed on the site with a small motor driven mixer, with the proportioning of the mix being with counted shovelfuls of each of the ingredients. Mr. McSherry had Jack gather rocks from the adjoining areas. Jack handed the rocks to his Dad, who dropped them into the forms to save on the amount of concrete used.

A happy time for the McSherry family was when the entire family assembled on the front porch in the evening. The porch was furnished with a swing and several chairs. Father and Mother and one or two of the children sat on the swing, the others sat on a chair or on the porch steps. The summer evenings were warm and quiet. Mr. McSherry would light up a cigar, as he explained it, to keep the mosquitos away. They observed the neighborhood and made conversation.

Today a penny is not worth anything, but in the thirties it would purchase a handful of candy. One day, as happened occasionally, Mom gave each Bill, Dave, & Jack a penny to go to Kline's store for some candy. Because Jack was smaller, Mom gave his penny to Bill to carry because Jack may lose it along the way. So Bill was carrying two pennies in his closed hand on the way to the store. Along the way, he discovered that he only had one penny in his hand instead of two. He had lost one of the two. So, they went back home and Bill told Mom that he lost Jack's penny. Generously, Mom gave them another penny to take its place and they went to the store and purchased their candy.

One day the group of friends walked to George Bailey's property and followed the creek to its source which was a large spring. The spring was swampy with cattails growing in and around it. There were many frogs in the pond. Bill, Dave, Jack, John Cook and Jack Llewellyn found an old tin, five-gallon can nearby. They gathered handfuls of frog eggs from the pond and put them into the can which was partially filled with water. They carried this can, with the frog eggs in it to the McSherry home and put it in the back yard. After a few days, the eggs hatched and the can contained many tadpoles swimming around. Over time, the kids watched the tadpoles develop legs, and eventually became little frogs. In that area, the little frogs were called "juggies". The juggies grew larger. Then it happened. During the evening and all night, the juggies
would chirp at a very high pitch, very loudly. This went on for several nights, then, Mrs. McSherry ordered the juggies to be taken back to the swamp on the Bailey farm. This was done immediately.

In the wintertime, quite often Sunnyside would receive heavy snows. This was always fun for the kids, but the adults had to go to work. Dad always drove his car through the snow to get to work at the silk mill in Shamokin. In the evening, when he returned to Sunnyside, he had to drive up a steep hill to get home. They did not have four wheel drive at that time, and the wheels would spin as they slid on the snow on the uphill grade. It seemed that there was always a crew of men and boys at that location when the snow was heavy, and as the cars spun trying to go up the hill, this group of men and boys would get behind the car and push it up the hill. This was a typical cooperative spirit of the people during the depression.

In their early years the McSherry kids did not read much, except as necessary in school, however, they did purchase, for five cents, in the stores of Shamokin, books called "Big Little Books". The big little books were small books, 3 ½" x 4 ½" x 1 ½" thick. They usually contained a little over 400 pages. With each turn of the pages, on the right page there was a picture about the story with a caption beneath describing the event. On the opposite page was a continuation of the narrative concerning the story. In reading these books, Jack did not see the need to read the narrative, all he had to do was to look at the pictures and read the explanation under the picture and he felt he knew the whole story.

Big Little Books of the 1930's

Mom and Dad each had subscriptions to some of the published magazines. They relaxed in the living room in the evening and read these magazines. Dad subscribed to the Saturday Evening Post and the National Geographic Magazine. Mom read the Ladies Home Journal. Some of the other magazines of the time were Colliers, Popular Mechanics, Country Gentlemen, and Good Housekeeping.

The Good Housekeeping Magazine
Dated October 1933

This cover of the Good Housekeeping Magazine depicts some children bobbing for apples. This was a form of entertainment at many parties, especially Halloween parties. The apples were floated in a tub of water. The kids had to lower their heads down to the water surface, and without the help of their hands, they had to pick up the apples with their mouth and teeth. This was very difficult to do.

Sometimes, while going through the five and ten cent stores in Shamokin, the kids would purchase toy soldiers. The price for a painted, lead, toy soldier was five cents. Over a period of time, the kids collected quite a few of these soldiers. There were many different types of soldiers, including infantry, machine gunners, navy, artillery, and even cowboys and Indians. The soldiers would be set up in their chosen locations and imagination created the rest.

Toy soldiers

Collection of toy soldiers
1930's

Cowboys and Indians

There would be occasional baseball games played on a baseball field in Overlook. The field had three bases (rocks) placed in the proper locations, plus the home plate. The entire infield was reasonably level and raked to a rather smooth surface. A backstop screen was erected behind the catcher consisting of log posts with chicken wire attached. The outfield was irregular and contained weeds. These games were local kids, the older ones, against teams from other nearby areas. One of the players, the pitcher, was Earl Chaundy. Earl was better known as "chair", supposedly because he liked to sit. "Chair" was a great pitcher, striking out many of the opposition players. However, "Chair" did not do much fielding, only pitched. If a fly ball came close to him, he would walk over and catch it, but he never ran to catch a ball passing near him. Everyone liked "Chair" and appreciated him for his great pitching ability.

Another member of the Overlook team was Delmar Bailey. Delmar didn't always hit the ball when he was at bat, but he certainly had a mean swing. Delmar was the son of Mr. & Mrs. Elwood Bailey who had the farm directly behind the McSherry home. Delmar was in the Navy during World War Two. He was on board a destroyer in the battle of Okinawa, which was attacked by Japanese suicide planes known as kamakazies. The ship was hit by one diving plane, but fought on. They shot down several additional suicide planes, then they were hit again by another kamakazi. Badly damaged they continued to fight back. Finally they were hit by a third kamakazi whereby the ship rolled over on her side and sunk stern first into the ocean. Delmar Bailey went down with the ship, a major tragedy.

It should be noted that Bill McSherry was in that same battle with Delmar Bailey, but not on the same ship. Bill was on board a Battle Cruiser. Bill survived the war.

The political atmosphere, during the Great Depression, was probably pretty hot, but the kids in their Paradise did not pay much attention. The only way they did participate in the politics was during the local elections when people were running for all of the miscellaneous local offices. Each candidate would have a card printed showing the office they were running for, along with their party, probably their picture, and, of course, their name. All of these cards were the same size, and they were distributed generously throughout the neighborhood. The kids would collect as many of these cards as they could. Then the games started. Two, or more kids, each having their handful of voting cards, commonly called "voties", would take turns laying down a card face up. When the last name of the politician of the last card laid down by the one person was topped by a card having a politician's name starting with the same letter, this player was the winner and would pick up the entire pile of cards.

Another card that the kids collected was picture cards of the mid-1930's Japanese attacks on China. These were found in packages of bubble gum which could be purchased at Kline's store in Sunnyside for one cent. The sheet of bubblegum was the same size as the card. These pictures were rather brutal. One example was a picture of planes bombing school busses resulting in fiery scenes.

Jack 1938

Occasionly, the family would go to Shamokin to the movies. Dad liked the Tarzan, Frank Buck, and Will Rodgers movies. Mother liked the Shirley Temple movies. So those were the movies that they went to see. At times, the Tarzan movies became quite frightening to little Jack. If a lion attacked toward the audience, or if the savages got nasty, Jack would push up against his Mother who soothed him by telling him that it is only a movie. After the movies, they always drove to Martz's ice cream parlor and got very large ice cream cones.

During the 1930's, Mr. McSherry was in the Navy's Fleet Reserve. This required him to go to Philadelphia, and probably to the Navy Yard, periodically for training activities. Sometimes, when he went to Philadelphia, he would take his family along. The entire family, including Dad, who had the evening off, would stay overnight in a hotel. This was an experience for the kids, because all night long they would hear the street noises, which included the clanking of the street cars. That was strange compared to the chirping of crickets at night in Sunnyside. In the hotel, there was an elevator to take the people to the upper floors. The interior of the cabin of the elevator was quite small, possibly four feet by five feet, plus or minus, in area. It had a brass folding grid to close it when the passengers were inside. The elevator had an operator who controlled the grid door and the movement of the elevator. As the McSherry family approached the elevator, the operator came out to greet them. He had a big smile on his face as he approached the family. At this point, young Jack hid behind his Mother and was making loud objections. It happened that the operator was a black man and the only black people that little Jack had ever seen were in the Tarzan movies. As a result, Jack, who was probably about four years old, shouted "I'm not getting in that cage with that savage!!" The elevator operator was a very nice man, still smiling, he talked to young Jack to calm him down. With a little coaxing, Jack got into the elevator, and all was well.

Upon the invitation of others to visit or go to some get-together, Mr. & Mrs. McSherry would hire a local girl, Mary Sanders to babysit for the three boys. She was a dependable, and compassionate girl, however, on one evening of babysitting she apparently angered little Jack, which was not hard to do, and Jack said to her "I will kick you up in the air and when you come down you will be dead!" Most likely Mary just laughed it off. However, about seventy years later, Jack was attending a reunion of people who attended the Mount Union School. Mary Sanders' sister,

Alda, was attending the reunion. Jack's son, Jack III was also in attendance. When Alda and Jack III got into a conversation, Alda told him that when Jack was a little boy, he was a brat. Jack III enjoyed that, and reminds his father of it on many occasions.

Social activities would occasionally take place at the local fire company, locally known as the hose house. Some of the activities were for the whole family and sometimes only for the adults. The fire company was founded by local residents in the early thirties. Some of these people were Jack L. McSherry, Oscar Dockey, Clarence Boughner, Herbert Knoebel and Clair Leisenring. Of course there were others also. The fire company had two fire trucks. One probably dated back before the 1920's and had solid rubber tires. The other was a little newer and had air inflated tires. The fire alarm system was unique. It was located outside in front of the hose house. There was a log framework with the outer rim of a large locomotive wheel hanging from it. The wheel was split at the bottom, probably to improve the sound. Alongside the wheel was a small box attached to the post with a sledge hammer in it, with the handle hanging from the box toward the ground. When there was a fire, a person would get the sledge hammer out of the box and strike the locomotive wheel with hard swings of the hammer. The clank of the impact created a very loud sound and would be struck repeatedly until the firemen arrive. That alarm could be heard miles from the hose house.

The Hose House
Photo dated 2017

One time the McSherry kids, and some of their friends, were playing around in Overlook in the early evening. Overlook is at a higher elevation than all of the other areas around it, so, with the good visibility, they noticed a fire in Irish Valley, which is several miles away. They determined that it was a building burning, so they rode their bikes down the hill to the Hose House to sound the alarm. Just as they got to the Hose House, a car came speeding up and a man jumped out. With help from the kids, the man took the sledge hammer out of the box and began pounding on the locomotive wheel. Immediately volunteer fireman arrived from different directions, some in cars and some on foot. The firemen opened the doors of the hose house, went inside and got into the truck. They tried, but the truck would not start. The kids immediately went behind the truck and pushed it out of the Hose House and down a short hill in front of the hose house. The fire truck started on compression and the firemen raced to the fire. The building that was burning belonged to the Galen Clark Meat Processing Company.

In the days of the depression, viewings and funerals were held in the homes of the deceased. While the body was on display in the home, there would be a bouquet of flowers attached outside to the front wall of the house adjacent to the front door to notify the public of the event. In the early thirties, Jack's great aunt died. She was the wife of Mrs. McSherry's mother's brother. In the evening, Jack, his brothers, and several friends had planned to stay overnight in the scout cabin, which was located in a wooded area in Overlook. Jack's mother instructed Jack to go to the viewing of her aunt before going to the cabin. Why just Jack? Apparently the other members of the family went to the viewing earlier in the day while Jack was off wandering in the woods. Jack obediently walked to Weigh Scales, opened the front door, walked inside directly to the casket, looked at the body, said nothing to anyone, and left. He then walked to the cabin in Overlook.

The scout cabin was a wood frame structure, probably about twenty five feet long and fifteen feet wide with no interior partitions, just a large open space. It had a wooden floor and at the one end was a large stone fireplace. The fireplace was built by Oscar Dockey. Early in the evening, the boys fooled around, played "weak horses", roasted hot dogs in the fireplace, and after more fooling around, found their beds and prepared to go to sleep. At about this time, during the rowdyness, one of the kids picked up one of Bob Clifford's sneakers and threw it across the room. The sneaker landed right in the middle of the fireplace where a hardy fire was burning. Needlessly to say, the sneaker disappeared in the flames. The next morning, Bob wrapped his foot in some old rags and walked home. There were no beds in the cabin, nor was there any furniture. The kids placed blankets on the floor. That was their bed. Except Jack. Jack slept on a 12" wide by 8 foot long wooden bench attached to one of the sidewalls.

The game of weak horses was mentioned as one of the events of the evening in the scout cabin. For this game, two of the boys would take turns choosing from the group who would be on their side. Once the teams were established, one team would form the horse and the other team would be the jumpers. The horse group would take their positions. One would stand with his back against the wall to cushion the head of the first horse from smashing against the wall. The remainder of the team would bend over, with their legs erect and hold firmly onto the legs of the horse in front of them, thus forming a long, flat surface of backs. The team of jumpers would take turns jumping onto the backs of the horse. To do this, they would get a running start and jump as far as they could onto the horse. Once on the horse, they had to hold their position. When all of the jumping team were on the horse, the horse would either firmly stay up, or they would collapse under the weight. If the horse held the load, they would get their turn to jump. However, if the horse collapsed, they would remain as the horse for another round.

As part of his working with the boy scouts, Oscar Dockey set up a get-together one evening at the scout cabin. The main event of that evening was to make a large kettle of mulligan stew and then feast on it. Dockey instructed each of the kids, prior to the event, that they should bring along to the cabin a tin cup, a spoon, and a can of any vegetable or similar food item that they would like to bring. Dockey brought a large kettle in which he had a soup bone and some broth, which he cooked at home, to serve as a basis for the stew. Dockey collected the cans of various ingredients, opened them one by one and poured the ingredients into the kettle, which was simmering over the coals of a hot wood fire. There was a good variety of vegetables, canned soups and other ingredients that went into the stew. One unusual proposed ingredient was a can of fruit cocktail. Dockey held that can up, looked at it quizzically, nodded his head, and poured it into the stew. After the mulligan stew was well cooked, each of the kids got their cup full of stew which they ate with great delight, and there was plenty of stew so that everyone could go back for more. Dockey was a good cook and always made good food. The mulligan stew was excellent and will be remembered always by all of the kids who had the privilege to eat it.

The United States mail was delivered every day, except Sunday, to the residents of Sunnyside by Mr. Rodarmel, the mailman. The McSherry mailbox, # 442, was located along the main road through the area and at the intersection of the entry road into the development, along with the mail boxes of many of the other people in the neighborhood. Mr. Rodarmel put the mail for the McSherrys in their box promptly at 11:00 in the morning on each delivery day. His schedule was flawless. The McSherry's address was RD#2 Box 442, Shamokin, PA. Rodarmel delivered the mail, in his early 1930's car from the Shamokin Post Office. The walk from the McSherry home to the mail box was about one-quarter mile.

The Shamokin Post Office (Now abandoned)
Photo dated 2017

CHAPTER 2
MOUNT UNION SCHOOL

The elementary school for Ralpho Township, which included Sunnyside, Weigh Scales, Overlook, and a great portion of the countryside adjoining these areas, was the Mount Union School of Overlook. The school originally had two classrooms and two teachers for the eight grades, but in 1931, an additional two classrooms, and two teachers were added to the building. Bill started going to the school in 1931, Dave in 1932, and Jack in 1933. Jack started school at the age of five. Apparently his mother needed a break. Each school year started on the day after Labor Day. Because the school was in a rural area, the school term was only eight months, rather than the customary nine months, so that the children would be available at home early in the spring, usually May 1st or 2nd, to work on the farm. The McSherry family did not live on a farm, so they gained an extra month of summer vacation, as did most of their friends

The school day was started with the teacher, or an assigned student, going to the outside and ringing a hand-held, brass bell, thus notifying the students that it was time to enter the school and be seated at their assigned desk.

The brass school bell

Mount Union School
1939

The Mount Union School had four classrooms, four teachers, and eight grades. To make these conditions work, they had a system. The classes started at 9:00 AM, had a 15 minute recess in mid-morning, then a one-hour lunch break. In mid-afternoon, there was another 15 minute recess, and dismissal at 4:00 PM. Class sessions were one-half hour long. Since there were two classes in each room and only one teacher, the teacher would teach the one grade while the other grade would work on their assigned studies. After the half hour session was over, the teacher would switch to the teaching of the other class and the class she had been teaching would work on their assignments. The one class was seated at one side of the room, and the other class at the other side of the room.

The school day would always begin with the students standing alongside their desks and reciting the Lord's Prayer. This was followed by the pledge of allegiance to the flag. The pledge of allegiance, at that time, did not include the words "under God", which were added to the pledge in 1954. The pledge of allegiance had certain procedures that were carried out while it was being stated. To start the pledge, the students placed their right hands over their hearts, and when they made the statement "to the flag", they extended their right arm forward, palm up, toward the flag and held it in that position until the pledge was completed. The students would be seated, and after the teacher read several verses from the Bible, classes would begin. This was a public school and followed the same procedures as all public schools.

When Bill started school, the rest rooms were outhouses. There was no plumbing in the school. The next year, the plumbing was put into the boy's rest room and the girl's rest room, which were added to the school in the addition of the year before.

During the time that the McSherrys went to that school, the following teachers taught there. Bill and Dave had some teachers that left the school before Jack got there. Bill & Dave had Mildred Adams for the 1st and 2nd grades, and Miss Hope Richards for the 3rd and fourth grades. Otherwise, their teachers were the same as Jack had, as follows; Jack's 1st and 2nd grade teacher was Jemima Eltringham, his 3rd and 4th grade teacher was George Vought, his 5th and 6th grade teacher was Evelyn Brunner, and his 7th grade teacher, and the principal of the school, was Dorothy pensyl. The McSherrys moved from Sunnyside while Jack was in the 7th grade. However, Miss Pensyl taught both the 7th and 8th grades.

When Jack was in the first grade, every afternoon at about three o'clock, the teacher had the class go to the blackboards which covered the entire rear wall, and front wall of the classroom. Classes for the day were over at four o'clock. However, for quite some time, each time that the class was sent to the blackboard, Jack went to the blackboard but just stood there participating in nothing. The teacher would ask him if he was sick and he would answer "yes". So the teacher told him that he could go home. Jack was not sick, just bored, so he would leave school and happily run all the way home. This went on for quite some time until the teacher finally figured it out and changed the procedure.

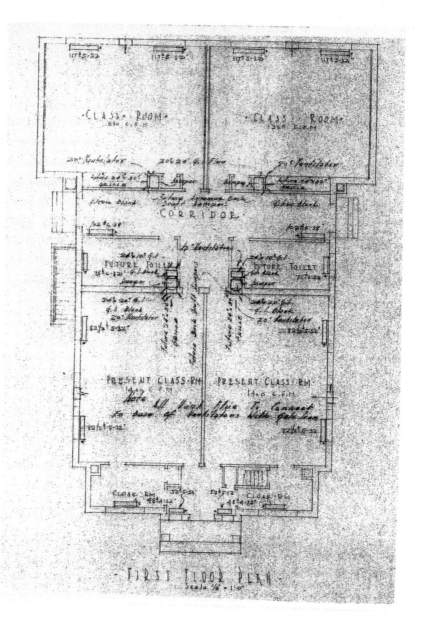

Although not totally clear, this is a photo of the original blueprint, prepared in May 1930, for the construction of two classrooms, a corridor, and two rest rooms to be added to the Mount Union School. The addition was constructed in 1931.

The kids carried their lunch to school each day, some in brown paper bags, and others in their metal lunch buckets Lunch consisted of a sandwich, usually baloney or summer sausage, or sometimes jelly, along with a piece of cake and possibly an apple. They ate their lunch at their desks, and as soon as they finished, they went outside to play.

To clean the blackboards, the school had stiff backed erasers which had a soft material for the erasing surface.   Periodically when the erasers had in them an abundance of chalk dust, the teacher would designate two people to take the brushes outside and clap them. Clapping the brushes consisted of taking a brush in each hand and clap them together. This would create a cloud of chalk dust. The clapping of the two brushes would continue until they created no more dust. Then two more brushes would be put through the same procedure until all of the brushes were clean. The brushes then would be returned to the little shelf at the bottom of the blackboards. At the end of the day, the blackboards would be cleaned with a wet cloth. The teacher usually did that herself after the kids went home.

One day, when Jack was in the first grade, he opened his lunch bucket and it was loaded with small ants. Miss Eltringham noticed and came to his assistance. She checked through the lunch and pulled out certain things that she said were allright to eat, and gave them to Jack. She cleaned out Jack's lunch bucket while he ate the rescued food.   It was determined that the ants got into the lunch when Jack was preparing to leave home to go to school, and had temporarily set his lunch bucket on the concrete walk where many ants lived.

When in the first grade, at the age of five, Jack was rather immature.   This one day, as he sat at his desk, his teacher, Miss Eltringham, was talking to the class on some subject of learning. Jack was bored and would rather have been outside, in the woods, and possibly climbing a tree. As a result, he was not paying attention to the teacher. In his boredom, he chewed the eraser off of his wooden pencil leaving the twisted metal casement of the eraser at the end of the pencil. He then proceeded to rotate the metal tip of the pencil on the top of his brand new desk making circular scratches over the entire top of the desk.

Upon observing the scratches on Jack's desk, Miss Eltringham became much distraught and left the room in search of Miss Pensyl, the principal of the school. Upon finding Miss Pensyl, both ladies returned to the classroom and stood over Jack, as he sat at his desk, and excitedly discussed the resultant scratches. After some discussion and observation, they brought a bottle of liquid from which they applied the liquid to the entire top of the desk with a soft cloth. In Jack's opinion, the surface of the desk looked much better, and the scratches were less pronounced. However, the teachers concluded that the desk did not look good, and proceeded to tie Jack's hands together behind his back, and made him stand in the corner at the front of the classroom. Jack's instructions were to face the corner, but instead he faced the class with a rebellious look on his face. He was to spend the remainder of the class day in that corner.

After some time, Jack was able to slip his one hand from the bindings and thereafter stood facing the class with his arms hanging down and with a piece of rope hanging from the one arm. Jack was wearing his high top shoes which had on the side of one of them a little pouch that contained his pocket knife. The kids in the class thought that Jack bent down and got his pocket knife out and cut the bindings. This, of course, was not true, but he allowed them to believe that. This incident was apparently forgotten and forgiven because Jack's parents were not notified, nor was there any further repercussions.

When Jack was in the second grade, Miss Eltringham had a spelling bee for her students. Jack came in first in the contest . Miss Eltringham gave him his prize, a small porcelain doll holding several pencils. It seems that she was pretty sure that a girl would win the bee. Jack accepted his prize graciously.

George Vought
3rd & 4th Grade Teacher
Mount Union School
May 6, 1940

George Vought

George Vought taught the 3rd and 4th grades beginning in 1935. Mr. Vought was the only male teacher in the school. He always had a long stick in his hand, or available, if necessary. He was a disciplinarian and a good teacher. He kept the class awake and attentive. Some took his methods as overly brutal, but he always had traces of a smile when he performed his disciplinarian procedures, and he never overdid it or showed any anger. He was liked and appreciated by most of his students. Some of his methods of punishment would be termed as brutality by today's society, but no one was ever hurt. Nor were there uncontrolled interferences in the classroom by rowdiness. Society today should possibly take note of his methods and realize that teachers cannot teach unless they have complete control in the classroom. Some of Mr. Vought's procedures are as follows. If a child was fooling around in the classroom, Mr. Vought would walk up behind him and give him a swat on the seat with his big stick. If a child was extremely unruly, he would take him out to the cloakroom and paddle him on the seat. Punishment for some offense in the classroom could consist of having the student stand in the front of the classroom with his arms extended outward to the side. He would then put a book in the upward palm of each of the student's hands. The student would stand there in that manner for about fifteen minutes. If the arms began to sag, he would swat the student on the seat with his stick and the arms would straighten. When the students took a spelling test, if they incorrectly spelled a word, they had the option of writing the word ten times, or come to the front of the classroom, bend over, and get a swat on the seat with the paddle for each word misspelled. No child screamed or cried during these methods. Some even laughed, as did the class. Society today would be in horror over the preceding, but in those procedures, George Vought never hurt anyone, he maintained discipline, and he was an excellent teacher. In addition, Mr. Vought was never seen to strike a girl with his paddle, nor did he inflict any of his other methods of discipline on any of the girls.

One day, when Jack was in the third grade, the school had a visitor, who was apparently a medical salesman. This person gave each of the students in the 3rd and 4th grades a sample tin of "666 Salve". The container of the salve was a small tin about the diameter of a half dollar, and less than a quarter inch thick. This was a very strange happening, because it was not the customary event of the day. This tin contained a black salve, but Jack does not know what it was for, or even why he got it. It was apparently sanctioned by the school. When they got the salve, one of the students opened the tin, stuck his finger into the salve, and licked it off of his finger. He proclaimed that it was good to eat. Therefore, jack and quite a few of the other boys did the same. Jack ate the entire contents of the tin. No one received any ill-effects, nor was there ever any follow-up concerning the event.

When Jack was in the fourth grade, and Mr. Vought was the teacher, Jack was wearing a bowtie which had a stretch band around the neck to hold it in place. Jack moved the bowtie from its proper location and placed it on the top of his head. Then he made funny faces at his friend, Harry Harper, who was sitting nearby. Apparently Mr. Vought decided that this was not proper procedure during the class sessions. Unknown to Jack, Mr. Vought came walking up to Jack, from behind, and swatted him on the seat with his long stick. Jack was then told by Mr. Vought to sit with the girls. Mr. Vought had all the girls sitting on the one side of their half of the classroom, and the boys sat on the other side. He did not specify which girl Jack was to sit with, so Jack sat with the girl of his choice. That was the only time that Jack was ever swatted by Mr. Vought's stick.

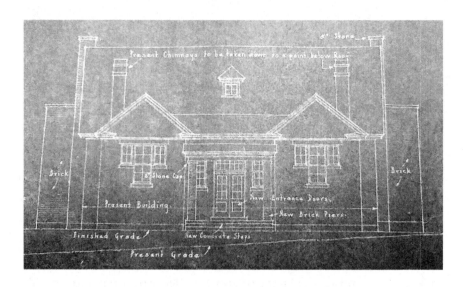

Architect's sketch of the West Entrance to the Mount Union
School
Dated 1930

The entrance to the school which led into the classrooms of
George Vought and Evelyn Brunner was on the west side of the
building.

On the outside, this door was approached by going up several
concrete steps to a covered portico. The door was within that
portico. The exterior wall, adjacent to, and above, the door was
made of red brick, as was most of the school.   At the left jamb of
the door and about three feet up from the concrete floor, there
was a brick which had a thumb print in it. The kids used to put
their thumb into the print then pull it out and state, "look what I
did!" The thumb print was apparently put into the soft clay by a
workman at the brickyard before the brick was baked.

The use of that building as a school ended around the mid 1960's
and sometime after that had been sold to a church congregation,
Grace Chapel. In the Spring of 1975, the congregation
commenced adding a church sanctuary, to the side of the school,
and at the same time converted the inside of the school into
classrooms and offices. In 1975, Jack was an adult. As he drove

by the school, he stopped to see what the workmen were doing. He learned that the entire front of the school was going to be covered with building materials, completely covering the special brick forever. So, he talked to the construction foreman and told him about the brick. The foreman gave Jack permission to remove the brick and even loaned him the tools to do it. Jack chiseled out the brick and took it home. That special brick is shown in the photograph that follows.

The brick with the thumbprint

School recesses and the lunch hour were time for schoolyard fun. The activities were never organized by the school, the children did whatever they would conjure up. Sometimes they played football, or baseball, or soccer, or the game of tag. Another favorite was to have "chicken fights". The smaller boys would ride on the back of bigger boys, then they would storm into a group of such combinations and try to knock the other riders off the backs of their "horses". It may be interesting to note that the children of this school never played basketball neither at school or at home. It was totally an unknown game to them.

Jack's teacher in the fifth and sixth grades was Evelyn Brunner. She was a dedicated teacher and a very pleasant person. All of the students liked her. One day, Jack and Wayne Taylor went outside during the recess, as all of the students did, but they went beyond the property of the school and into a woods through which a small stream flowed and fooled around in the water. Having fun, they forgot the time and went back into the school fifteen minutes late. Miss Brunner did not perform the George Vought tactics, but she delivered her own form of discipline. Wayne Taylor was required to write the word "revolutionary" two thousand times, and Jack was required to write the word "extraordinary" two thousand times. They had to write the words during recess and the lunch hour, and were not permitted to leave the classroom until they finished. Jack took his word list home with him after school one evening and wrote the words for a while. Then he persuaded his brother, Bill, to write the word several hundred times for him. It took days before Jack and Wayne Taylor finally completed their work.

When Bill was in the seventh grade, Dorothy Pensyl was his teacher. One day Bill was outside at recess when Miss Pensyl came storming out a nearby exit from the school with an angry look on her face and carrying a big stick. Bill thought that she was looking at him, so he ran away as fast as he could. However, Miss Pensyl walked rapidly in the opposite direction. She was chasing after Lester Carl, who quite often amused himself by annoying Miss Pensyl.

Bill had another schoolyard problem about that same time. He and other kids were throwing snowballs. Bill threw a snowball at Dave, but missed, and the snowball went through the window of the girl's restroom. Bill was basically a good student so, therefore, he did not get into any trouble for the incident.

When in the sixth grade at the Mount Union School, Jack had a folding pocket magnifying glass. The glass was hardly ever used to look at small objects. Jack's main enjoyment of the glass was to focus the sun on an object and watch it burn. While sitting at his desk, as Miss Brunner was explaining things to the class, the sun happened to be shining on Jack's desk from a nearby window. So Jack took his magnifying glass out of his pocket and proceeded to burn his initials into the top of the wooden desk. The smoke was pouring from the burning desk, however, even though the smoke should have been obviously noticeable by sight and even the smell, Miss Brunner never noticed. There was no further mention of the initials after that.

Typical school desk

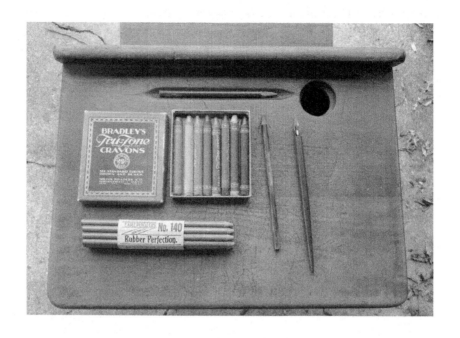

This photo shows the top of a vintage school desk, with crayons, erasers, pencils and a pen, from the Great Depression era. Note the hole to hold the bottle of ink.

Miss Evelyn Brunner
5th & 6th Grade Teacher
Mount Union School
May 6, 1940

Miss Evelyn Brunner

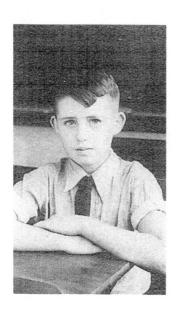 

Bill   Dave

Jack

School Pictures

1936

Girls playing during recess
Mount Union School

One of the requirements of the Mount Union School was that, every month, each student had to memorize a poem and recite it to the teacher. The poem was the required monthly poem from their poem book, and this applied to every student in every grade in the school. Jack was not interested in the poems, he disliked them, and as a result he recited them very poorly, or possibly never memorized them at all. One evening, Jack's mother tried to help him to memorize one of the poems. She would read it to him and had him repeat it, but he just did not get it memorized. In reading the poem to jack, she came to one line which said "Be not like the dumb driven cattle", after which she blurted out "you dumb cow!" She was not a nasty person, so as soon as she said it, she burst out laughing. Jack laughed too. It is our understanding that, to this date, Jack refuses to read, or even look at, any poetry

Memory Selections
For Pupils
of the
Elementary Schools
of
Northumberland
County

Odd Years' Series

Grade 2
Suppose

Suppose, my little lady,
  Your doll should break her head,
Could you make it whole by crying
  Till your eyes and nose are red?
And wouldn't it be pleasanter
  To treat it as a joke,
And say you're glad " 'Twas Dolly's
  And not your head that broke?"

Suppose your task, my little man,
  Is very hard to get,
Will it make it any easier
  For you to sit and fret?
And wouldn't it be wiser
  Than waiting like a dunce,
To go to work in earnest
  And learn the thing at once?

—Phoebe Carey

Grades 3 & 4
The Wonderful World

Great, wide, wonderful, beautiful world,
With the beautiful water about you curled,
And the wonderful grass upon your
  breast—
World, you are beautifully dressed!

The wonderful air is over me,
And the wonderful wind is shaking the
  tree;
It walks on the water and whirls the mills,
And talks to itself on the top of the hills.

You friendly earth, how far do you go,
With wheat fields that nod, and rivers that
  flow,
And cities and gardens, and oceans and
  isles,
And people upon you for thousands of
  miles?

Ah, you are so great and I am so small,
I hardly can think of you, world, at all;
And yet, when I said my prayers today,
A whisper within me seemed to say:
"You are more than the earth, though
  you're such a dot;
You can love and think and the world can-
  not."

—William Brightly Rands.

Grades 5 & 6

The Charge of the Light Brigade

Half a league, half a league,
  Half a league onward,

TWENTY-TWO

All in the valley of Death
  Rode the six hundred.
"Forward, the Light Brigade!
Charge for the guns," he said:
Into the valley of Death
  Rode the six hundred.

"Forward the Light Brigade!"
Was there a man dismay'd?
Not tho' the soldier knew
  Some one had blundered:
Theirs not to make reply,
Theirs not to reason why,
Theirs but to do and die:
Into the valley of Death
  Rode the six hundred.

Cannon to right of them,
Cannon to left of them,
Cannon in front of them
  Volleyed and thunder'd;
Storm'd at with shot and shell,
Boldly they rode and well,
Into the jaws of Death,
Into the mouth of Hell
  Rode the six hundred.

Flash'd all their sabres bare,
Flash'd as they turn'd in air,
Sabring the gunners there,
Charging an army, while
  All the world wonder'd:
Plung'd in the battery smoke
Right, thro the line they broke;
Cossack and Russian
Reel'd from the sabre-stroke
  Shatter'd and sunder'd.
Then they rode back, but not,—
  Not the six hundred.

Cannon to right of them,
Cannon to left of them,
Cannon behind them
  Volley'd and thunder'd;
Storm'd at with shot and shell,
While horse and hero fell.
They that had fought so well
Came thro' the jaws of Death,
Back from the mouth of Hell,
All that was left of them,
  Left of six hundred.

When can their glory fade?
O the wild charge they made!
  All the world wonder'd.
Honor the charge they made!
Honor the Light Brigade,
  Noble six hundred!

—Alfred, Lord Tennyson.

TWENTY-THREE

Report Card 1

Report of O... Mc Sherry   **First** Grade
For the year commencing September 5, 19 33 **and ending** May 4, 19 34

THE Teacher Requests	MONTH	N Days Absent	Times Tardy	Conduct	Reading	Spelling	Writing	Drawing	Arith-metic	Lan-guage	Geogra-phy	History	Physi-ology				Signature of Parent or Guardian
That parents keep their children in constant and punctual attendance.	September	1		C	C		B	B	C	C			C				J.L. McSherry
That they oversee home studies.	October	0		C	C+		C-	B	C+	C			C				J.L. McSherry
That they visit the schools.	November	2		C	B		C-	O	C+	C			C				J.L. McSherry
That they examine and sign this report as often as presented.	December	0		C+	B		C	B	B	C+			C+				J.L. McSherry
	January	4		C+	A-		C+	C	A-	C+			B+				J.L. McSherry
Note:— In Deportment and Studies, 90 to 100–Excellent; 80 to 90–Good; 70 to 80–Medium; 60 to 70–Doubtful; below 70–Failure.	February	0		A-	A		B	C+	A	B			A				J.L. McSherry
	March	0		A-	A		B	C+	A	B			A				J.L. McSherry
	April	0		A-	A		B	C+	A	A			A				
	May																Promotion Second Grade
	June																
	Average			B	A-		C+	C	B+	C+			B				

Jemima Eltringham, Teacher.

Report Card 2

Promoted to Sixth Grade

Report of Jack Mc. Sherry   **Fifth** Grade
For the year commencing Sept. 7, 1937, **and ending** may 6, 1938

THE TEACHER REQUESTS	MONTH	Days Absent	Times Tardy	Conduct	Reading	Penman-ship	Spelling	Arithmetic	Geography	English	History	Health	Music	Drawing	Civics	Room	Signature of Parent or Guardian
That parents keep their children in constant and punctual attendance.	September			C	A-	B-	B+	B	B	B	B+				D		J.L. McSherry
That they oversee home studies.	October			C	A-	C	A	C	B	B	B+		B	B			J.L. McSherry
That they visit the schools.	November			C+	A	B	A	B+	A	A-	B+		A	A-			J.L. McSherry
That they examine and sign this report as often as presented.	December			C+	A	A	A	C+	A-	B+			A	A			J.L. McSherry
	January (MID-YEAR EXAMS.)			88	90	100	92	94	96				88			Av. 95	J.L. McSherry
METHOD OF GRADING	February			B	A	A	A	A	B-	B+			A	A-			J.L. McSherry
A–90 to 100–Excellent	March			C+	A	A	B	B+	A-	B+			A	B			J.L. McSherry
B–80 to 90–Good	April			B+	B-	A	A	B-	B	B			A	B			J.L. McSherry
C–70 to 80–Medium	May			C	A	A	B+	B	A	B			A	A			
D–60 to 70–Doubtful	June (FINAL EXAMS.)			100	70	97	90	84	91	92			80			Av. 88	
E–Below 60–Failure	Average			C+	A	A-	A-	B-	B+	A-	B-		A-	A-			

M. Evelyn Brunner, TEACHER

In comparing Jack's first grade report card with his fifth grade report card, there is a great improvement. You must realize that Jack started school when he was five years old, and apparently quite immature. Of course, Jack's grades in conduct were never very good.

While in the seventh grade, Jack sat next to an organ which happened to be in that room to accompany any singing that may take place. To play the organ, it was necessary to pump the foot

74

pedals to force air through the bellows. The organ had a defect in that when the organ was setting idle, if someone pumped air into the organ for a brief period, about five minutes later, it would let out a loud roar. Jack enjoyed pumping air into the organ about five minutes before the class started.

As Christmas approached, the school children began getting excited. The teachers waited until about two weeks before Christmas, then they would spend about a half hour every day singing Christmas carols and songs. In addition, each teacher would work up a Christmas program of some sort which, when ready, the parents were invited to come to the school for the program.

Every Valentine's day, the teachers would set up a decorated box, with a slot in the top, at the front of the classroom where the students could insert Valentine's day cards for their friends. Mrs. McSherry always had her kids put a card in that box for every child in the class.

It is interesting to note that the schooling during the depression was very simple. All the children needed was a simple school building, a desk, books, a tablet of paper, a pencil and a dedicated teacher. This is what they had, and it seems that their education was way superior to the education provided by the giant schools of today, with all of their electronic contraptions.

The schools were operated by the County with guidance from the State. According to the United States Constitution, the schools are to be governed by the State. Even though the schools are none of the federal governments business, today we have a Federal Department of Education.

This Valentine is typical of the cards of the depression era. This particular Valentine was sent by Jack via US Mail to David Burrell, Jack's uncle, on Valentine's day in 1933. The card was retrieved at an auction at the Burrell house after David Burrell died in 1992.

The school district contracted for one school bus for Ralpho Township. The bus was owned and operated by Clarence Mensch of Elysburg. Mr. Mensch lived across the street from the Ralpho Township High School.   In the morning, on school days, Mr. Mensch would drive his school bus out of Elysburg and into the countryside from which the kids attended the Mount Union School. At various locations along the way, he would pick up students, some of them having walked a half-mile, or more to the bus stop. Mr. Mensch would deliver the kids to the Mount Union School. After unloading all of the grammar school kids from the bus, he would begin loading high school students from Weigh Scales, Sunnyside, Overlook and the nearby rural areas on the bus. He would then drive the same route to the High School in Elysburg, picking up students along the way. The same system was used to haul the kids back home after the schools were dismissed.

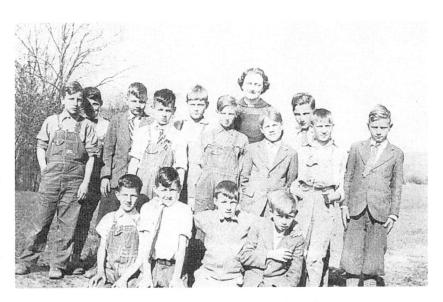

Fifth and sixth grade boys   1937
Front row, left to right: Russell Horn, Dave McSherry, Bob Clifford, Unknown. Second row, left to right: Claude Drumheller, Bill McSherry, Joe Morris, Donald Spayd, Russell Koons, Bill White, Jack Zelinsky, Howard Hartzel, John Cook, Richard Morris. Teacher: Evelyn Brunner.

Bill McSherry, John Cook, Bob Cllifford 1937

David McSherry, Lois Hill, Betty Fredrick, Bill McSherry
1937

CHAPTER 3
GAMES, ACTIVITIES, AND ENTERTAINMENT

Children of the Great Depression innovated to amuse themselves. Sure, they had some toys, or baseball equipment that their parents purchased for them, but they also devised their own games and made their own equipment and toys.

One of the games that they played every spring as soon as the frost left the ground was "nips". All it took was an old broom handle and they could make their own equipment. The nip was a piece of a broom handle about five or six inches long, with points carved on each end. They pointed the nip with their pocket knives, which they always carried. Then they made a handle of the necessary length, depending on the height of the child. The end of the handle would be carved flat on both sides for several inches on the bottom. With the nip and handle carved, they were ready to play the game. A circle was scribed in the ground about 30" in diameter. The batter would stand by the circle while the pitcher, who is about 30 feet away, would throw the nip and try to get it in the circle. If he got it in the circle, the batter would be out. If the nip landed on the line, the batter would get one chance to hit the nip, and if it landed free of the circle, the batter got three chances to hit the nip. To hit the nip, the batter would hit the point of the nip with the edges of the flattened end of the handle to cause it to bounce into the air, then he would follow through and try to hit the nip with the handle to send it as far away from the circle as he could. Taking his three allowable strikes, in the same manner, he would move the nip as far away from the circle as he could. Upon completion, the batter would then state that he will take ten points, or whatever amount that he thought that he could get away with, for his hit. The first challenger, the pitcher, would attempt to travel from the nip to the line of the circle in ten large steps, exaggerated by jumping. If he arrived at the line in ten steps, or less, he would get ten points, and would become the batter, and the present batter would be out with no points. If he failed to make it, the next player in line would try. If anyone would make it, he would become the batter, and the game would continue. If all failed to make it, the batter would get ten points, and would bat again. Of course, the person with the highest score won the game.

Another game that they played was "piggy in the hole". Piggy in the hole equipment included an evaporated milk can and a club for each player. The club was about 3 to 4 feet long made from a broom handle or a stick from a tree. It was played with a large hole in the center and smaller holes along the periphery, one less than the number of players, usually three or more. The smaller holes were about eight to ten feet from the center hole. The game started when one of the players, usually the biggest kid, hit the milk can as hard as he could to drive it away from the large hole. The players would then put their sticks in the large hole and walk around a circle until someone, usually the biggest kid, would yell "piggy". Players would then rush to put their stick in one of the smaller holes. The one who did not get his stick in a hole had to go and get the can and try to drive it into the large hole with his stick. If he got it into the hole, he was the winner and got to hit the can for the next game. However, as he was bringing the milk can toward the hole, any of the other players could take their sticks out of the small hole and hit the can away to deter the other one from getting it in the hole. While he was swinging at the can to drive it away, the person trying to get the milk can in the hole could put his stick into the small hole and that person would then have to try to put the milk can in the hole.

There was never time for fear or other problems for the children in this paradise. The lands around the McSherry house area were used to throw a baseball back and forth, or to play a baseball game called "strike, pitch and catch". This game only required three people to play; a batter, pitcher, and catcher. The ball that was used was a rubber ball. The pitcher would throw the ball to the batter who would strike at it. He may hit it or strike at it and miss. The batter would be out if he struck three times and missed the ball, or if he swung at the ball and missed and the catcher caught it on the first bounce. The batter was out if he hit the ball and the pitcher caught it on the first bounce. Then the catcher would move up to be the batter and the pitcher would become the catcher. The batter who got out would be the pitcher. If the pitcher should catch a fly ball, the batter is out and changes places with the pitcher.

Behind Bill & Dave and their wagons
Is Mr. McSherry's 1930 Graham.

Other activities were cops and robbers, which had much running around the area with guns drawn, and a lot of hollering. Similar to this was cowboys and Indians. Even Alley Oop was mimicked. They made stone axes by splitting the end of a cut tree limb, then putting a suitable flat rock in the split and wrapping it with rope or string. Bill was always Alley Oop, Dave was King Guzzle, and Jack was Foozy. Others like Harry Harper, or Wayne Knoebel would be Dootsy Bobo. There was never a lack of imagination or ingenuity. None of the children in the area had elaborate possessions or toys. They did not need them. With their imaginations they created their own games, made their own toys, and kept busy on the basis of their own ingenuity.

For entertainment, they made a form of dart which consisted of a dry corncob with three large chicken feathers pushed into the pulpy center of one end of the cob. This dart was thrown as hard as possible which would cause it to spin and soar for quite some distance. It was a fun toy to play with. Another fun, but dangerous, device was a form of arrow projection. The arrow was made from a piece of a wooden barn shingle. A piece of the shingle, about two inches wide was split from the shingle. A 2" x 2" tail was formed at the thin end of the shingle for several inches, then tapered to a shaft width of about ¾ inch for most of the length of the shingle. At the end of the shaft, at the thick end of the shingle, an arrow head was carved, then a small notch cut into the side of the arrowhead. The arrow is now finished. To project this arrow into the air, a device was made to shoot it. This device consisted of a short limb or broom handle to which a piece of rubber about ½" wide and 4 inches long, cut from an innertube, was tied to the broom handle or limb. A string loop was tied to the outside end of the rubber strip. The shooter would insert the loop of string into the notch of the arrowhead, then stretch the rubber strip, aim and let it go. The arrow could fly hundreds of feet and penetrate whatever it hit. That made for very good pastime.

Tires during the depression were totally open on the side that was set into the wheel. To enable them to be filled with compressed air, an innertube, made of rubber, was inserted inside the tire. Air was then pumped into the tube with a hand pump until the tire was properly inflated. Since the tubes were made with very flexible rubber, the kids would take an abandoned innertube and cut a cross-section out of it, thus it became a large rubber band. These rubber bands, or strips, were used to make slingshots and other useful gadgets.

Every spring, it was time for each kid to make his sling shot which he would carry and use the rest of the summer. The first step was to find a tree with a symmetrical wye in a ¾" diameter limb. Then cut the wye from the tree. Rubber strips, about ½" wide and 4" long would be cut from an old innertube and attached to the two prongs of the wye by wrapping the rubber around the branch then tying it tightly with string to hold it in place. At the other end of the rubber strips, a leather square which was cut from the tongue of an old shoe, was slotted at two edges of the square. The rubber strips were slid through the slits and tied with string to hold them. The slingshot is now finished. A suitably sized rock would be placed in the leather pouch, the rubber strips stretched, then let go and the rock will soar through the air at great speed. The slingshots were dangerous, but fun to shoot. Notice that, in making these things, they used their pocket knives which they carried with them at all times. Pocket knives were considered as tools and were carried by all men and all boys. They were never considered as weapons as they are today. Young Jack had his own pocket knife when he was three or four years old.

Another devise that was made by the kids were guns that shot rubber bands. The first ones made consisted of a short board about 4" wide and possibly a foot long. A clothes pin was attached to the back of the gun with two rubber bands that wrapped around the front of the gun and around the clothes pin, thereby holding the clothespin in place. To load the gun, another rubber band would be folded and one end inserted between the clothes pin and the gun. The other end of the rubber band would be stretched to run around the front of the gun. When the clothespin was depressed at the bottom, the top would open and the rubber band would project off the gun toward the target. The rubber bands could be purchased in a store, but usually were cut from an innertube.

As time passed, the rubber band rifle was invented. To do this, a plank about 4" wide and four feet long would have square notches, spaced several inches apart, cut into the rear end of the top of the board. A long strip of leather, about ½" wide, cut from an old leather boot, or jacket Would have one end nailed to the top of the gun several inches in front of the most forward notch. Then it would be fed down into the notches and to about six inches beyond the back of the gun. Rubber bands, cut from innertubes would be stretched from the front of the gun then placed into the notch on top of the leather strip. The rubber bands would be shot from the gun by pulling up on the leather strip, firing one rubber band at a time.

The McSherry kids each had a BB gun at a very young age. The BB's came in a tube and were usually purchased at Hacks Hardware Store in Shamokin. The BB guns were dangerous if not used carefully. They were mostly used to shoot at tin cans, bottles and other forms of targets. .

A gentler form of entertainment was to make a parachute. A piece of cloth about 12" square, or a handkerchief, was the basis for the parachute. A piece of string about 12" long would be tied to each corner of the cloth, then a rock, or small toy soldier, would be tied to the end of the four strings. The parachute would be loosely rolled up and thrown into the air as high as possible. In the air, the chute would open and glide to the ground.

As has been mentioned, the kids always found ways to amuse themselves, which brings to mind the fun of walking on metal shoes. The reader is familiar with tin evaporated milk cans. With the milk cans laying on the ground, the kid places his shoe centered on the side of the can and presses down. The top and bottom of the can bend in toward the foot. Then the kid stomps his foot with the can loosely attached and makes it fit tighter. Doing this with both of his feet, he now walks around clanking with each footstep. Now isn't that a fun way to spend an afternoon?

The kids discovered how to build stilts. They would cut two trees or tree limbs, which were about two inches in diameter and six feet long. Two feet from the bottom, they would nail a piece of wood to the side of the post. This piece of wood would project about three inches and was about four inches deep. The person would mount the stilts by holding the poles upright, place one foot on the projection on the one stilt, then leap forward and place his other foot on the second stilt. He was now on the stilts and must maintain his balance. With much practice, he would be able to walk with ease for great distances. Once a person learns to walk on stilts, he never forgets how. The kids had fun walking on these stilts many times and many distances.

One summer, the McSherry kids and their friends decided to build an underground hut. They chose a location, to the east side of the driveway to the garage, where a future road was excavated. This provided an embankment about three feet higher than the future road surface to the adjacent land. This entire location was probably twenty feet off of the McSherry property line, but nobody cared. From the level of the future road, they began digging a narrow trench into the bank. This trench, which was to become the entrance to the hut, was narrow, but wide enough for a kid to crawl through. This entry trench was about three feet long. Then the excavation widened as they dug out a space about five feet long and three feet wide. At this point they decided to excavate another room to make the hut bigger. They excavated another trench out of the right side of the first area, several feet long then flared it out to make another room about five feet by five feet. When they got the spaces to the depth and area that they wanted, they found a large rock on the one sidewall of the second room. They excavated around this rock to expose the flat top of the rock. This would be their fireplace. At this point, they gathered whatever lumber they could find around the area. They even found a large door. The longer lumber was placed on the ground to span across the openings. The door was placed flat on top of the pieces of lumber to close up the space. The smaller scraps of lumber were placed over the other larger pieces of lumber. When all areas were covered with lumber, they shoveled dirt onto the lumber to totally conceal any trace of the hut. To further hide the hut, over a period of time weeds and grass grew over the hut. In addition, a short piece of stove pipe was installed over the fireplace and through the roof of the hut. The only visible parts of the hut that could be seen from the outside was the entrance tunnel and the stovepipe. It was rather eerie to see smoke from a stovepipe coming out of the ground. This hut was a meeting place, and gathering place for the kids for a long time after it was constructed.

In the year 1938, Oscar Dockey, who was the superintendent of the Shamokin Cemetery, hired a group of the Sunnyside-Weigh Scales kids to work in the cemetery. As Memorial Day approached, additional help was needed to get the cemetery looking its best. The helpers consisted of John Cook, Bill McSherry, Dave McSherry, Jack Llewellyn, Marlin Snyder and Jack McSherry. These kids mowed the grass, cleaned the inside of mausoleums, and even helped to dig graves. They worked hard and did their work well.

The McSherry's cat, "Dopey", is getting a drink of water from a watering place, in the back yard of the McSherry residence, made from a broken and abandoned high tension electric insulator, which Mr. McSherry found in a field just east of the McSherry home.

As the boys grew, they determined their own way to build wagons for themselves. The big dump near Weigh Scales served as their location to acquire the materials needed for the project. The basic piece was a large board, about twelve inches wide and possibly four feet long. At the rear of the plank, and on its underside, they would nail a 2 x 4 laterally across the full width of the plank. Incidentally, the nails used for this project also came from the dump. They were usually rusty and bent, but they were straightened to do the job. An axle, which was a round rod about ½ inch in diameter, was attached to the 2 x 4 with a series of nails driven into the 2 x 4 against the axle. Then the nails were bent over and around the axle to keep it in place. The axle extended beyond the ends of the 2 x 4 far enough to receive the wheels. The ideal wheels for a wagon were large ones that came from a baby carriage, or a tricycle. These were also available at the dump. The axle had a hole through it at each end where a cotter pin could be placed to hold the wheel onto the axle. However, the kids never had any cotter pins, so they would insert a nail through the hole and bend it so it would stay in place. The attachment for the front wheels of the wagon was the same as the rear, except that the 2 x 4 with the axle attached was connected to the board with a bolt, washers and nut so that it could be rotated for steering. The wagon could be steered with the feet by placing the feet on the front 2 x 4 and pushing one side or the other as necessary. Or, a rope could be attached to each side of the front 2 x 4. The driver held the other end and pulled on the rope on the appropriate side to turn the wagon. Over the years, many of these wagons were constructed, some simple and some enclosed with big cardboard boxes to appear as automobiles.

Photo of a wagon made to look like an automobile.

In the background is the garage that Mr. McSherry built
for the neighbor.

Also in the background is a house under construction which
Mr. McSherry helped build.
1937

Wayne Knoebel on his wagon
1938

A favorite social event, but a relaxed get-together, was a corn roast. A fire would be started at a suitable location, then freshly pulled corn would be placed in metal trays over the fire, with wet burlap surrounding the corn, which was still in the husks. In this manner, the corn was roasted until well done and hot. When ready, everyone would get an ear of corn, husk it, then put butter and salt on it. The corn would be eaten off the cob. There was always enough corn so that everyone got their fill.

Similar to this was the weenie roasts. A small fire, or fires would be built. Sticks several feet long would be cut from nearby trees, and, with a pocket knife would be pointed on one end. A hot dog would be pushed onto the pointed end of the stick. Then, the people would sit around the fire, holding their sticks with the weiner on it so that the weiner was over the hot coals of the fire. When totally roasted and heated, the dog would be removed from the stick, put into a bun with mustard or ketchup added. A hot dog cooked over a fire, with friends and conversation all around, made a tasty and happy evening. Further, to add to the variety of food, it was common to roast potatoes in the fire. Mostly the potatoes were just put into the coals. Of course this would result in a layer of burned potato skins and some potato. This blackened outside would be removed and the soft, well-cooked potato could be eaten. With a little more effort, before building the fire, a hole could be dug under the area of the proposed fire. The hole could then be lined with rocks, the potatoes placed in the hole, then covered with small rocks. At the right time, the potatoes could be dug out. The potatoes would be well done, but contain no burned areas.

Dad, Beah the dog, and the three sons on a sled in the year 1930

In the wintertime, when the big snows came, the sleds would be taken out. There were many hills, of varying steepness, all around the area. Some were simple and gentle and others were steep resulting in high speeds and the necessity for good steering. The McSherry kids were fortunate enough to have a large bobsled with a hood and steering wheel. On the back of the sled was a handle which when pulled acted as a brake by forcing metal teeth to grind into the snow or ground. This sled was probably designed for about four kids, however, the McSherry kids managed to get as many as eight on it as it roared down the hill. The way they did this was to have Bill sit at the steering wheel to drive, Jack was assigned to sit in front of the steering wheel, facing back straddling the hood and the steering wheel. Four others sat on the sled by squeezing themselves into position. The last two sitting on the sled sat on the handle of a shovel, with the square shovel extending back beyond the end of the sled. Dave usually sat on that shovel. The last person stood on the extension of the rungs of the sled at the rear of the sled and held on to the persons sitting on the sled. Bill was a good driver and usually managed to go around the curves as necessary. The sled overturned some times. In addition to the bobsled, each kid in the neighborhood had his own sled, so there was always much activity on the streets and hills in Sunnyside when the snow arrived.

1937

The McSherry kids also had skis. They did not see the need to carry the ski poles with them, so they skied without them. They did not have much ability to steer the skis, but chose hills that did not require too much steering. Some of the hills were very steep and the rides were very fast. They discovered by leaning they could turn the skis a little, however, in the event of a tree or other obstacle in their path, the problem was solved by simply sitting down and eventually stopping.

Other wintertime activities were snowball battles, the building of forts or igloos, and of course, building snowmen. There was no insulated clothing at that time, so the customary way to keep warm was with long johns, two pairs of pants, a shirt, sweater, coat, and hat, plus possibly a scarf. The feet were vulnerable to getting cold. Socks as thick as would fit into the shoe were worn, then the shoes were wrapped in newspaper and inserted into the boots or galoshes. Usually the feet got cold, and quite often numbed, but the kids very seldom gave up their fun in the snow until it was time to go home.

Winter also was the time for ice skating. Most of the kids had ice skates, the kind that clamp to the shoes. Unless they traveled by car or bicycle to a dam or pond, the only place to ice skate in Sunnyside was in the swamp just below the house and on the other side of the Pennsylvania Railroad. The railroad had several sidings in that area to make up the trains, so in order to get to the swamp, it was usually necessary to crawl under one or several railroad cars to get to the other side. Once at the swamp, the skates would be put on and skating began. The swamp was only about two feet deep but served very well for skating. In addition, the swamp was in a wooded area, so there were trees growing through the ice. This made skating interesting by weaving between the trees.

Harry Harper lived in a house a short distance below the McSherry house. He spent most of his waking hours with the McSherry kids. He joined in with all the activities, whatever they were. Harry was a close friend around home and at school.

In the summertime, as Independence Day was arriving, all of the stores stocked fireworks, including Kline's store in Sunnyside. The kids began buying these fireworks about a week before the holiday. The stores stocked all kinds of fireworks from sparklers to cherry bombs. The favorites for the McSherry kids and their friends were some firecrackers about 1 ½ inches long and possibly 1/4" in diameter. They were semi-powerful. To light the fuse on the firecrackers, they used punk which, when lighted with a match, just had a smoldering, non–flaming burning area. Punk could be purchased in the stores along with the firecrackers. The store-purchased kind of punk was a round wire with something attached that smoldered when lit. The kids did not need the store type of punk. They got their punk in the woods. The punk was dried fungus attached to an old stump. The kids would pry the punk from the stump. This was good punk. It would smolder all day without reducing much in size. The 1 ½" firecrackers would make a loud bang, and if placed under something, it would send the object flying.

One day at dusk, the kids were lighting this type of firecracker while holding it in their hand. After lighting it, they would throw it out in front of them. And watch it explode. One time, Jack wasn't paying proper attention, lit the fuse, and forgot to throw it. It went off in his hand. Two of Jack's fingers and his thumb were numb for quite a while afterward.

At another time, Bill, Dave, Jack and John Cook were exploding the same type of firecrackers. Bill and John Cook took one of the firecrackers and pushed it into a small hole in the side of the garage, then lit the fuse. When the fuse burned to within a quarter inch of the firecracker, the fire went out. Bill and John discussed it and each one said they were not going to relight the fuse. Jack stepped in and said he would light it. He had a plan. The firecracker was fairly close to the corner of the garage, so he determined that he would reach around the corner with his punk and light it. He did this, but unfortunately he also looked around the corner. He touched the fuse with the punk and it exploded immediately. Fire flew and burned a small hole in Jack's face less than an inch below his eye. No adult was ever consulted about the burn, and Jack just allowed it to heal by natural processes. Perhaps the decision to outlaw firecrackers in Pennsylvania was a good idea. It keeps fireworks danger away from foolish kids.

They were free and happy. The kids at that time would spend all of their time outside. They did not have television, or computers, or cell phones to entice them to spend their lives uselessly loafing around the house. The only device in the house that may create a reason to stay in the house was the radio. However, the only programs that the McSherry kids listened to were "Little Orphan Annie" and the "Lone Ranger." And even these programs were listened to only if they were not away from home climbing trees or doing other useful things.

Little Orphan Annie Cup

Dave & Bill on their bicycles with their BB guns slung over their shoulders.   1936

On March 14, 1938, young Jack got a bicycle for his birthday. He tried riding it, as most kids do, with bad balance. Besides, his legs were not long enough to push the pedals all the way down. So he rode and crashed a lot for those first few days. Finally, he got on to it and was able to ride the bike with his brothers and the other kids. The bicycles were transportation to everywhere. They were used to go to Overlook to play baseball, to ride to Weigh Scales to visit friends, to ride to Shamokin, to ride to one of the swimming holes, to ride into the countryside, and even to Uncle Calvin's cottage near Bear Gap. They were also ridden to nowhere just for fun. On one occasion, Jack and his friend, Wayne Taylor, were riding their bikes on a dirt road in the countryside, both pedaling at full speed. Wayne was about fifty feet out in front of Jack. As Jack was going down a hill, pedaling at full speed, his wheels dropped into a rut in the road which was formed when the road was muddy, but now the soil was solid as a rock. This caused the bike to run out of control and Jack flew horizontally across the handlebars and landed on his stomach in the middle of the road.

Wayne Taylor did not notice and kept going. Apparently Jack was knocked out for a while because when he woke up, there were two farmers standing next to him. One said that he saw Jack fly across the handlebars and land on the road. He said to Jack, "I thought that I would find you dead !" Wayne Taylor came back, and the two of them started toward home, which was a little over a mile away. The front wheel of Jack's bike was shaped like a pretzel, so he lifted the front end of the bike off the ground and pushed it all the way home. As he approached the house, his Dad saw him coming with the twisted wheel and said, "What did you do this time?" Anyway, shortly thereafter, Jack's Dad took the wheel to a bicycle shop and had it straightened.

During the Depression, most of the rural roads were dirt roads. The Township had the responsibility to maintain those dirt roads that did not belong to the State. To do this, they would pull a drag along the road with a tractor or a truck to smooth the surface. The drag was usually homemade, consisting of iron blades attached to a timber frame. After the road was graded, they sprinkled used crankcase oil onto the surface to keep down the dust.

Mom's brother Calvin had a cottage along the Roaring Creek at Bear Gap. The McSherry kids always liked going there. They could play in the creek or run around in the woods. When they were little, they would go there with the family for outings. Later, they would go there, with Uncle Calvin's permission, on their bicycles. Sometimes they would sleep there overnight, and other times they may stay there for a week. Sleeping in the cottage was an experience when the wild cats would scream nearby in the woods. On one occasion, they saw some hunters in the adjoining field. Jack decided that he was going to scare the hunters, so he took the bear rug, which Uncle Calvin had on his living room floor, and wrapped it around himself with the snarling head over him, and he went outside and peered around a tree and growled at the hunters. Apparently he did not scare the hunters, and fortunately they did not shoot him.

Uncle Calvin had an organ in the cottage. It had foot pedals on it to pump air into it to make it play. He also had a Victrola. The Victrola was in a waist high cabinet. The top was hinged to get to the operating mechanism, and to put the records on the turntable. To make the Victrola play, there was a crank on the side of the cabinet to wind it up. Once wound up, the record was put on the turntable and the needle arm was lowered to put the needle on the record, then the beautiful music came out of the Victrola.

Jack, Dave, Bill
At Uncle Calvin's cottage
1935

Uncle Calvin played the piano and was an all-around good guy. He had a good sense of humor and was always fun to be around. He would visit the McSherry family often and was greatly appreciated.

To the kids, music was not one of the great items of interest. However, Uncle Calvin attempted to teach each Bill, Dave, and Jack to play the piano. Bill did reasonably well and was playing the piano quite well, but he never pursued it in later years. Dave advanced fairly well but never really became a piano player. Jack had little interest and never practiced. He preferred climbing trees to practicing the piano. Jack liked to listen to good music from the radio, so he did take some interest in music. Some of the popular songs of the mid 1930's were "Playmates" and "The Woodpecker Song". Those two songs were directed toward the kids, but they were big hits. The music, both Popular and Country, of the depression era was melodious and pleasant to listen to, as compared to the music of the twenty-first century. The vocal music of the twenty-first century is basically a prominent drumbeat accompanied by a screaming lady. Merriam-Webster's dictionary describes music as "The science or art of pleasing, expressive, or intelligible combination of tones". Screaming to a drumbeat cannot be considered as a pleasing, expressive or intelligible combination of tones.

Calvin Burrell   1930
Uncle Calvin was always a flashy dresser

During the depression years, every Sunday, the McSherry family would get in the car around 10:00 in the morning and would drive out to Grandfather and Grandmother's home at Bear Gap. It is interesting to note that they had assigned seats in the car. Dad drove, Mom sat alongside him in the front seat. Bill sat on the right of the rear seat, Dave on the left, and Jack in the center. All through the depression, and wherever they went, that was the seating arrangement. They would arrive at the Grandparents' house around 10:30.

As they drove up to the house, Grandmother was always seen sitting in her chair in the kitchen, at the window, watching and waiting for them to arrive. Usually the entire Burrell family was home, including the Grandparents plus Sons, Calvin, Bertlette, and David. Also included was Bertlette's girlfriend, Ruth Bird, up until 1933. After 1933, she was Ruth Burrell.

Each one of the three sons, who, of course were the uncles of the McSherry Children, had their own points of interest. Calvin was a cheerful man, and as a result, comical. He always had interesting stories to tell, he played the piano, and he enjoyed entertaining the kids. Bertlette was the ingenius type. He was a school teacher, and he enjoyed woodworking with his jigsaw and other mechanical tools. He would make toys for the kids and furniture for the adults. David liked the outdoors and enjoyed taking the kids for hikes in the woods.

Two of Uncle David's L. L. Bean catalogs for outdoorsmen
Dated Spring 1932 and Fall 1932

It should be noted that Bertlette had the first power driven lawn mower in the area. In the mid 1930's, before power mowers were on the market, he mounted a small gasoline engine on the top of his hand pushed reel mower and connected it to the wheels of the mower. The engine made the mower move and when reel mowers moved, the blades would rotate. Thereafter he mowed his lawn with this power mower.

Grandmother would prepare and serve dinner at noon. In the evening, she would prepare and serve supper. In the winter time, it was usually after dark when supper was served and the Burrell home had no electricity. They ate supper with the light of a kerosene lamp setting in the middle of the table. After supper, the family would gather in the living room, also in the light of a kerosene lamp or two. In the late evening, the McSherry family would get back into their car and drive back home to Sunnyside.

Another great accomplishment of Bertlette's was to install an electric light system in the house. He purchased a small generator and connected it to a bank of batteries. With this power, he wired the entire house with this low-voltage system and provided lights at the most appropriate locations in the house. He would recharge the batteries about once a week with his generator. This lighting system was used in that house for many years until sometime in the 1940's, when the power company provided electricity to the house.

During the day, the kids had the freedom to do whatever they wanted to in the vicinity of the Grandparent's home. There were large areas of pine trees nearby which were planted by the Water Company. The trees were close together, so, because of a lack of sunlight the lower limbs on the trees were dead. The kids broke the lower limbs off to make paths through the pine trees. They created a large maze of paths and amused themselves accordingly. Travelling a little farther away from the house, through the woods, they would walk down to the #2 Dam, the one that their Dad helped to build. It was a large dam and was very deep. Alongside the spillway from the dam was an excavated bank of rock. In that rock bank were many small quartz crystals which the kids would pry out and take home. They would also find small pieces of rock which contained many crystals.

In the wintertime, they would ice skate on the dam, usually with their Dad's or an uncle's supervision. On a windy day, they would open up their coats and hold them out to their sides to form a sail. They would glide the entire width or length of the dam. However, it was hard work to skate back against the wind.

Uncle David owned a 1932 Plymouth coupe. The car had a rumble seat. A rumble seat is a seat for two located outside, to the rear of the cab of the car. It opened like a trunk lid, and the seat faced forward. When Uncle David took Bill, Dave and Jack for rides, Dave and Bill rode in the rumble seat, but Jack always had to sit inside the cab with Uncle David. Apparently Uncle David thought that Jack may stand on top of the rumble seat, or dance around on the seat and, perhaps fall out of the car. Jack never got to ride in the rumble seat.

A coupe with a rumble seat

Mr. John R. Steele, who lived in a rather large house in Overlook, was a typewriter salesman and repairman. Mr. Steele organized a Boy Scout Troop in the mid 1930's for the boys of the area, apparently to give them something positive to do so that they would stay out of trouble. The Boy Scout troop # 50 met every Thursday evening in Mr. Steele's home.   Mr. Steele did not necessarily follow all of the rules and procedures of the Boy Scout organization. The official age to become a boy scout was twelve years. Mr. Steele's troop had boys in it as young as nine years old. They would meet in a basement room of the Steele house. For the first hour or so, they would play board games, throw darts, play ping pong, or one of many other items of equipment furnished by Mr. Steele. This would be followed by an official meeting, with all of the members sitting in chairs around the large ping pong table. They had group recitations of the scout law, the scout oath, and the pledge of allegiance to the flag. Discussions would follow pertaining to possible projects of the troop, or going to summer camp. For those twelve years old, or older, he would have them take the test for tenderfoot scout. If they passed the test, and became a tenderfoot scout, he would give them a copy of the official Boy Scout Handbook, which he signed and dated for them. Obviously Mr. Steele purchased these handbooks at his own expense. Dues, five cents per person, were collected at every meeting for the treasury, hardly enough to pay any expenses. Tenderfoot scout was about the only rank that Mr. Steele pushed. There are many other higher ranks and merit badges that are available in the Boy Scout organization, but they were seldom mentioned at this troop. The only time that the kids would earn merit badges or rise in rank was when the troop went to Camp Nikomahs for a week or two in the summertime. Notice that the scout camp's name is Shamokin spelled backwards.

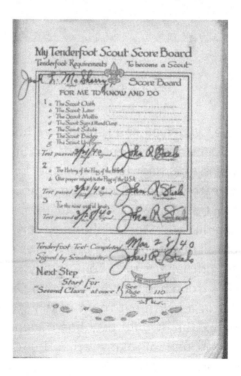

Jack's tenderfoot scout certificate

The members of Boy Scout troop 50 were divided into patrols. The patrols were usually named after wild animals, but the McSherry group named their patrol after an Indian Tribe. The patrol was named the Apache Patrol. The members of the Apache Patrol were John Cook, Bill McSherry, Dave McSherry, Jack Llewellyn, Bill Spotts, Jack McSherry, Jim Swift and marlin Snyder. The following picture shows the Apache Patrol plaque which Bill made to hang in the meeting place of the Apache Patrol.

The Apache Patrol treasury box

Jack was named to be the treasurer for the Patrol, so he made a wooden box to hold the treasury. During the depression, the stores had cheese in wooden boxes about 3 ½ inches wide, 3 inches high and about 12 inches long. The various pieces of the box were ¼" thick. You could buy the entire box or just a chunk of cheese out of the box. However, the kids would get these empty boxes, take them apart, and use the wood to make things. That is the wood that Jack used to make his treasury box.

Dad and Oscar Dockey became committeemen for the Troop. They helped Mr. Steele plan events and projects. The big money maker for the troop was the annual Bean Soup Suppers which were held in the Hose House. The bean soup was made by Mr. Dockey and was the best bean soup you could find anywhere.

Mr Dockey was the Superintendent of the Shamokin Cemetery. He was also a skilled stone mason. During the late 1920's, Dockey would haul home, in his pick-up truck, stones from the cemetery, including abandoned tombstones, abandoned curb stones, and any other cut stone that he could find that was no longer being used in the cemetery. Using these stones, and with his masonry skills, Dockey built himself a large, attractive stone house on a lot in Sunnyside. Dockey lived in that house for the rest of his life, and the house of tombstones still stands.

Oscar Dockey's house of tombstones
Sunnyside   Photo dated 2017

Every summer, a circus would come to Weigh Scales. They would arrive early in the morning in their big trucks. The McSherry kids, and some of their friends, would get on the roof of the McSherry garage and watch the colorful trucks arrive. They could see the activity well even though they were a mile from it.   However, after that initial view from home, they would go to the site of the circus and watch them set up. It was a very active operation. Workmen were tending to the animals, others were setting up the big tents. On one of these occasions, some of the kids were asked by the circus people to carry buckets of water for the elephants. Bill, Dave, John Cook, and a few others were selected. Jack and Wayne Knoebel were not selected because they were too little. Those selected kids carried buckets of water to the elephants for a longtime, but they were told that they would get free entry to the circus.   When circus time came, people were paying their fee and were entering the big tent.   The water carrying crew was walked to the side of the tent by the circus people who hired them.   When there, the circus people lifted the canvas tent up several feet from the ground, and told the boys to crawl in.   That was their free entry to the circus.   Jack's father and mother took Jack and Wayne Knoebel to the circus.

After the tents were set up, and before the circus started, there would be a circus parade from the site of the circus and up the highway to Tharptown and back.   The McSherry family would watch the parade by standing alongside the highway a short distance outside of Weigh Scales.   The elephants would walk along with big trucks carrying cages with lions and other animals. Clowns and other performers walked, and the circus band sat in a large truck playing circus music.   The parade was a very exciting part of the circus event.   The circus stayed at Weigh Scales several days, then they packed up and drove off for their next show.

The big dump was a short distance from the circus site.   One fall, some people went to the dump and were startled to see a twenty foot python crawling around in the dump.   The python obviously escaped from one of the circuses, but the escape was not reported.   The python was captured and placed on display in one of the show windows of the Montgomery Ward store in Shamokin.   He probably got a home somewhere, but the location is not known.

The milkman, who delivered milk to the Sunnyside area was also a hobby pilot.   This young man usually drove his milk truck as fast and wildly as he flew his small plane.   There was another young man, Kimber Lippiatt, who lived in Overlook.   Kimber built a glider in the barn behind his house, such project probably taking him a long time to construct.   One day, with the help of several of his friends, he took the glider out of the barn and pushed it to a long open field, which had a gentle slope from the nearby mountainside toward the village of Overlook.   A crowd gathered when the local people saw what was happening. Kimber and his friends had an old sedan, which they used to tow the glider up to the high end of the slope. At that point they aligned the glider with the sloping field, which was to become their runway. The sedan was attached to the front of the glider with a hook on the end of a steel cable. It was designed so that the hook would automatically unhook from the nose of the glider when the glider became airborne. Kimber chose his friend, the milkman, to pilot the glider. With everyone cleared out of the way, the sedan pulled the glider down the slope, picking up speed as it travelled. After travelling a great distance down the slope, and with the speed increasing, the glider lifted off the ground and soared into the air. However, unfortunately, the hook did not automatically release and the glider was anchored to the sedan. As a result, the glider did not rise any further, and veered to the right, and crashed into an apple tree. Neither the pilot nor anyone else was injured, but the failure of the flight was disappointing to all present.

Sunnyside had bus service to Shamokin. The busses ran through Sunnyside once per hour. The bus would leave the Shamokin railroad station on the hour, pass through Tharptown, Weigh Scales, Sunnyside and arrive at a turnaround at Overlook at twenty minutes after the hour. The bus would wait at Overlook until the half hour, then start its return to Shamokin. The fare from Sunnyside to Shamokin was ten cents. Some people walked to Weigh Scales to get on the bus because the fare from Weigh Scales was only five cents.

The WPA , a governmental Organization that provided work for the unemployed was mentioned earlier in this book. During the depression, there was another governmental organization that did good work. It was the CCC, Civilian Conservation Corps. The CCC hired young men in their late teens to their early twenties. They took the young men, by bus or in the back of a truck to their workplace. They usually worked on large projects, like building a dam, or planting trees, or even the building of roads. The young men would live in barracks-like buildings on the worksite. These young men received great experience in learning how to work, and they accomplished a lot. They were proud of their employment and worked hard.

In the later 1930's, all three McSherry kids, along with John Cook, Jack Llewellyn, and Donald Spayd each purchased a carbide lamp. The lamp contained two chambers, the lower one containing carbide and the upper one containing water. There was a lever to allow controlled dripping of the water from the upper chamber into the lower chamber. This mixture generated a combustible gas which forcefully exited a nozzle in the front through a reflecting area of the lamp. Similar to a cigarette lighter, the lamp had a steel wheel which, when rotated across a piece of flint, would make a spark which ignited the gas, thus the light was on. The group carried those lamps at night, and, in effect, played with them for their amusement.

After reading about the ingenuity of the kids of the depression, and how they responded to various problems of life without anger, but with determination and cheerfulness, is it no wonder that these children became the greatest generation and won the difficult fight of World War 2. ?

The McSherry Family, Left to Right
World War 2
Jack McSherry, Jr., David McSherry, Jack McSherry, Bill McSherry

CHAPTER 4
SHAMOKIN

When World War 1 was ended, Mr. McSherry was in France with the United States Navy. He was one of the people who organized the American Legion, and was a member of that organization ever after.

In Shamokin, on every holiday, there was a parade. Mr. McSherry put on his Navy uniform and paraded with the American Legion members. He enlisted his three sons into the organization entitled the Sons of the American Legion. The Sons of the American Legion went into the parades also. They followed directly behind the American Legion members each carrying a small American flag. The McSherry boys were members of the Sons of the American Legion from 1932 through 1936.

The sons of the American Legion
Shamokin, PA
1933

The Borough of Shamokin had two community bands. The one was called "Our band", and the other, "The Shamokin Band". They participated in all of the parades. No one got paid for participating in a parade at that time. They did it because they wanted to. In addition, there were the Shamokin High School Band and the Coal Township High School Band.

Independence Street
The Main Street and Commercial Center of Shamokin

Independence Street
Several years later

Usually Saturday was the day that the family would go to Shamokin to do their grocery shopping. The main street in Shamokin, Independence Street, would be lined along the curb with farmer's wagons and trucks full of produce for sale. Of course the grocery stores and other stores were also open for business. It was a treat to go to the food counter in Newberry's five and ten store and get a hot dog, with mustard, for five cents. Usually, as the McSherrys left Shamokin, they would stop at Henninger's bakery and get a still warm, freshly baked, loaf of bread. This would be eaten as soon as they got home as a special treat.

To purchase groceries in the larger grocery stores of the time was much different than today. The buyers would enter the store with their list of proposed purchases and wait in line for service. When their turn arrived, the clerk would take their list and accumulate all of their items on the list from the many shelves behind the counter, bag them, and collect the money and ring it through the cash register. Self-service stores were introduced to the grocery stores in Shamokin in the year 1938.

During the 1930's, Shamokin was the commercial and business hub for the local area and for the surrounding area. People from the surrounding towns would come to Shamokin to shop in the stores, to find employment, and for entertainment. Shamokin at that time was a borough led by a chief burgess. The town had three theaters, the Victoria, the Capital, and the Majestic. Also many dress and shirt factories, a very large silk mill, the F & S beer brewery, and one of the largest collieries in the area, the Cameron Colliery. In addition, Independence Street, the main thoroughfare in the town, was loaded with retail stores, hardware stores, three five & dime stores, restaurants, ice cream parlors and miscellaneous shops. All stores opened at 9:00 AM and closed at 5:00 PM, and they were always closed on Sunday. The restaurants and ice cream parlors stayed open well into the evening. Shamokin became a City in 1950.

One of the restaurants in Shamokin was the "Coney Island". The Coney Island was established in 1918 on Independence Street. This restaurant specialized in hot dogs, but had a secondary, hamburg, for those who insisted on eating them. (Yes, it was called a hamburg, not a hamburger.) The hot dogs were true Coney Island hot dogs, being grilled on a flat grill, placed in a bun, with a teaspoon full of the Coney Island secret sauce added. The hot dog was then topped with a heap of chopped onions. These were the best hot dogs ever made, and they cost only five cents each. At that time, almost every city in the United States had a Coney Island hot dog restaurant. Today it is difficult to find a true Coney Island hot dog. The secret sauce seems to have been lost.

The Coney Island

During the 1930's, only men worked in the Coney Island. They wore white pants and a white coat with long sleeves. To serve the customers, the waiters would place the hot dogs, side by side, on their arm, lined up from their wrist to well above the elbow, carry them to the table, then take them off their arm, one by one, and hand them to the customer.

Unknown to most people, during the Coney Island peak popularity in the 1930's, they had the onions delivered by the truck load. To unload them from the truck, they used a chute (like the coal truck deliverer's do). The chute extended into a basement window of the restaurant, and emptied into a pile in the onion bin. There was a lone man in that basement who spent all day, every day, peeling onions.

The Cameron Colliery

The Cameron Colliery was one of the largest mines in the Anthracite Coal Region. There were about 30 miles of tunnels in the mine, and the mine extended to a depth of 3000 feet.

The Eagle Silk Mill

In the 1920's, the Eagle Silk Mill was the largest textile manufacturing building under one roof in the United States. Built of brick, the building was seven stories high. Jack McSherry and Calvin Burrell worked in the dye department of the Silk mill in the late 20's and early 30's until they were laid off because of the Great Depression.

There were two hardware stores in Shamokin. Jones Hardware was the larger of the two. The other one was Hacks Hardware. The McSherry kids would buy their BB's at Hack's for their BB guns. When they got a little older, that is where they would buy their ammunition for their 22-rifle. At Hacks, as in all stores at the time, the customer would tell the clerk what he wanted and the clerk would get that item, bag it and ring it up in the cash register.

PENNA. GAME AND FISH LAWS
1933

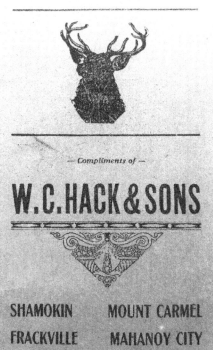

— Compliments of —

W.C. HACK & SONS

SHAMOKIN	MOUNT CARMEL
FRACKVILLE	MAHANOY CITY

Jones Hardware Store
Photo dated 2017

Jones Hardware was a much larger hardware store, the most interesting thing about Jones Hardware was their method of ringing up the sales. The cashier sat at his desk in his office in a balcony which existed over the sales area. There was a series of pulleys attached to the ceiling. Over these pulleys was a moving cable which travelled to the sales counters on the main floor. When a sale was made and the money received, the clerk would put the tendered money and a sales slip into a cylinder. The cylinder was attached to the moving cable and sent to the cashier on the balcony who registered the sale through the cash register, and sent the change and a receipt to the clerk below in the same cylinder. The clerk removed the change from the cylinder and gave it to the customer along with the purchased merchandise.

Mr. McSherry did his banking at the Guarantee Trust and Safe Deposit Company Bank in Shamokin. The building was a tall, granite building with high, round granite columns at the entrance. Inside, there was a high ceiling and stone walls. Along the one side was a wall containing windows for the tellers to look out from behind the wall. In front of these windows were metal bars which extended from the top of the window to within about three inches above the counter top. Business was conducted between the customer and the teller through that opening. While doing business, there was always friendly conversation between the teller and the customers, as though they were close friends. Banks at that time period opened at 9:00 in the morning and closed at 2:30 in the afternoon. The banks were closed on Saturday and Sunday.

The Guarantee Trust and Safe Deposit Company Bank
Photo dated 2017

The doctors during the Depression were family doctors. There apparently were no specialists. A doctor's office may include a father and son, but never a group of physicians. The family doctor would go to the homes of the sick patients to examine them and treat them, or the patient could choose to go to the doctor's office. Most people of that time saw a doctor only when they were seriously ill, or injured. They did not call the doctor for basic colds, or other minor illnesses. During the depression, Jack saw the doctor only a few times. He had his tonsils removed, when he was very little, at the doctor's office. His Mother consulted the doctor, who came to the McSherry house one summer, on two separate occasions, when Jack had poison ivy over his entire body from head to toe. On another occasion, the doctor came to the McSherry home and diagnosed David and Jack with the whooping cough. He gave them some mean tasting medicine which David took faithfully as specified, but Jack only took on occasion when he was forced to. Neither one of them went to the hospital nor stayed in bed, nor remained in the house. They went outside to play just as they always did. The coughing was ferocious. In spite of the medicine, they both got over the whooping cough in about three or four weeks. The McSherry's doctor was W. J. Harris of Shamokin.

The greatest fear of the mothers and fathers of the depression era was the outbreak of infantile paralysis (poliomyelitis, polio) in the mid-thirties. This disease was often fatal, or at least very crippling to the children who were afflicted with it. In late summer, all children were warned not to go swimming because it was believed that swimming contributed to the contraction of the disease. Even though infantile paralysis was occurring all across the nation, no cases of the disease are remembered to have occurred in the Sunnyside, Weigh Scales, Overlook area.

However, the common childhood diseases such as measles, mumps, scarlet fever, and chicken pox were relatively common. When a child had any of these diseases, their home would be quarantined and a poster was applied to their front door with the name of the disease on it. Scarlet fever was the most dangerous of these, but the measles was also somewhat dangerous.

In their younger years, all three McSherry kids developed cavities in their teeth. Mom took them to Dr. Robert M. Barthel of Shamokin. She chose Doctor Barthel because he used pain killing medicines and procedures which none of the other dentists used. When it was Jack's turn to have his teeth repaired, he was obviously frightened. When his teeth were being drilled, it was absolute torture. The drill, unlike modern equipment, rotated at a very slow speed, heated up the tooth, and pain was brutal. Dr. Barthel did his best with the equipment that he had, but the repair work was agonizing. Jack never went to a dentist again until he was seventeen years old and in the United States Navy. In the Navy, he was ordered and required to go to the dentist. Incidentally, the dental work performed by the Navy dentist, with much more advanced equipment, was totally painless.

CHAPTER 5
FOOD

All through the 1930's, the ravages of the great depression could be seen. People did the best they could to supply their families with food and other necessities. People were generous and would share food with the neighbors when they could. Even though things were difficult, the people did not complain. They just plugged on and worked wherever they could to earn as much money as possible to sustain themselves. Amazingly, even though people were poor, and many suffered because of this, there was no crime and no stealing. Toys or bicycles could be left anywhere outside and they were never taken. The quality and character of the people were of high standards.

During the depression, many heads of the household would travel to find work. They came from many far places, usually by hopping on a railroad car, then jumping off when they found a destination that may be helpful to them. These men would get very hungry. They would come to the various houses and ask for something to eat. All they wanted was a simple sandwich or other similar item. Almost everyone would accommodate them. Quite often they would offer to do small chores around the house to earn something to eat. Most people gave them the food without requiring work. Sadly enough these people were referred to as bums. It was not meant to be degrading or insulting. It was just terminology. However, it must have hurt to be in that category.

Breakfast mostly consisted of a bowl of cereal. As much as two spoonfulls of sugar were added to the bowl of cereal, then it was saturated in milk. The most common cereals at that time were corn flakes, wheaties, post toasties, puffed rice, puffed wheat and shredded wheat. Sometimes an orange would be added to the breakfast, but not very often. On one occasion, Dad peeled an orange and gave each of the kids one-third of the orange. Dad ate the peelings.

Mr. McSherry's younger brother, Raymond L. McSherry, lived in California. In 1933, Raymond and his wife, Nina, drove across the country in their 1930 Model A Ford coupe to visit the McSherry family in Sunnyside. They stayed with the McSherry family in Sunnyside for several weeks. Raymond was also a veteran of the Navy, so the two brothers had much to discuss. It was on this visit where Raymond, Jack, and Jack, Jr. took a ride in the Model A Ford and stopped at a place called the Colonial Inn located in the northern end of Tharptown. There they each got a bottle of Coca-Cola. This was the first time that Jack drank a coca-cola. Soft drinks at that time, and in that area, were called "temperance". They did not drink soft drinks, or soda, or pop. It was temperance.

The brush rows between fields contained wild cherry trees and raspberries. The kids could easily eat the raspberries. They also climbed the trees and ate their fill of cherries. Blackberries were abundant in the fields, which contained weeds and grass, but were not farmed. There was, at one location, a large patch of wild strawberries. The kids would pick these strawberries by the bucket full and take them home for strawberry shortcake. The wild cherries were much smaller than the commercially grown cherries, but they were a treat. The strawberries were smaller than commercial strawberries, and not nearly as sweet. The country kids always had their wild strawberries, but probably never ate a sweet commercial strawberry.

The kids, or Mom, would go out into the lawn areas in the springtime and cut dandelion plants loose from their roots and put them into a bag or container. Collecting many of these, they took them into the kitchen where Mom cleaned them, made a sauce, in which the dandelion was cooked. Dandelion made a good tasting meal.

Almost every home had its own grape arbor. When the grapes got ripe, the family members would gather under the grape arbor and pick bunches of grapes from the vine, and eat them. They would also pick additional grapes for Mother to use to make grape jelly.

Each summer, Mother made root beer. After making the root beer, she would put it in bottles and set it outside on the lawn in the sun to process it. This was excellent tasting root beer.

A good meal that Mom made was hamburger and macaroni, mixed with non–diluted canned tomato soup. The macaroni was first boiled and the hamburger was pre-fried, then they were added together, with the tomato soup, in the frying pan. This mixture was stirred and fried to perfection. Mom called it goulash. This same procedure could be made with spaghetti instead of macaroni, but then it was called spaghetti.

One evening, when Jack was about six years old, Mom was hosting a lady's get together. She had the table all set for a rather large group, then began setting dishes of various kinds of food on the table. One of these was a tray with many tuna salad sandwiches on it. Mom gave one to Jack, who was watching the proceedings. Jack took a bite and was elated. It was the best tasting sandwich that he ever ate. He had never tasted tuna before.

All of the meals in the McSherry family were eaten in the kitchen, except when they had company. They had assigned seats at the table. Perhaps they were not assigned, they just became traditional. One side of the table was against the kitchen wall. At the one end of the table was Dad's location, on the side opposite the kitchen wall sat Bill and Dave. Mom sat at the other end of the table. The kitchen table and chair set consisted of the table and four chairs. As can be seen, all of the chairs are now occupied. What about Jack? This situation was taken care of with a folding chair that was leaning in the corner of the kitchen. The folding chair was placed on the corner of the table between Dave and Mom. Jack always sat at the corner.

Occasionally, in the evening, Mom would make a tray full of chocolate fudge. The suggestion that this was going to happen created many cheers. All of the fudge was readily eaten before the evening was over.

In early fall, as did all the ladies in the area, Mom would can vegetables such as corn, string beans, among others. She also made jelly from whatever fruits or berries were available. This was stored on shelves in the basement and used when the occasion arrived.

 She also made pies, which were eaten instantly. (They did not have freezers during the depression). The best pie was the pumpkin pie. It was not necessary to eat the pumpkin pie with a fork and plate, the pie could be held in the hand with the thumb under the point of the pie, while the fingers supported the crust end of the pie. The pie was then held to the mouth and eaten from the point to the crust.

Mrs. McSherry's pumpkin pie was so good that the entire world is entitled to have the recipe. It is as follows:

Title: Ivy (Burrell) McSherry's Pumpkin Pie

Ingredients:
2 Eggs
½ Cup Sugar
1 Cup Stewed Pumpkin
3 Teaspoons Flour (Heaping)
1 ½ Cups Milk

Directions:
Beat eggs, add sugar, pumpkin and flour, Beat vigorously. Add milk and mix thoroughly. Pour into unbaked pie shell, sprinkle top with cinnamon or a little nutmeg. Bake at 400 degrees for about

15 minutes, then reduce heat to 350 degrees and bake about 45 minutes more, or until set.

She also made cherry pies, apple pies, shoofly pies, montgomery pies, and others. Then there were the cakes! She made a good cake called the hot milk sponge cake, and of course, she made chocolate cakes. Interestingly, on occasion, the chocolate cake would not raise when baked. When this happened she would say that the cake flopped. Jack liked it when the chocolate cakes flopped because when they did, they tasted like brownies, which did not exist during the depression.

The kids of the Great Depression never heard of pizza!

In the Shamokin area, they did not have green peppers. They were called mangos, and still are to this day.

Quite often, when the family went to Shamokin on a Saturday to do their shopping, they would stop at a peanut store where the peanuts were freshly roasted in the shell. They smelled extremely good and tasted just as good. The Sunday newspaper was always delivered on Sunday morning. This one morning, they still had some roasted peanuts left from the previous day. As he always did, Bill spread out the comic section on the floor, then laid down with it to read the comics. At the same time, he laid a handful of peanuts next to the paper, which he had previously shelled for eating as he read. He wasn't paying proper attention to the peanuts because, the family cat, Felix, sat alongside of Bill and ate all of the peanuts.

In Sunnyside, there was a small store where milk, bread, lunch meat, candy, ice cream, and other groceries could be purchased. The store was owned by the Kline family and was locally known as Klines. The store was located along the Weigh Scales to Bear Gap road directly alongside the Chaundy home. It was only a short walk for the kids to walk to the store from the McSherry home. One cent could buy several pieces of candy. Milk was ten cents a quart, and bread was ten cents a loaf. A cone of ice cream was five cents. They also had a gas pump at that store. At that time, the sign at the pump said gas fifteen cents per gallon, tax three cents per gallon, total eighteen cents per gallon. The gas pump was operated by turning a hand crank on the side of the pump. This filled a glass cylinder at the top of the pump. The gas then flowed from the glass cylinder by gravity through a hose and into the tank of the car.

At Kline's store they sold chewing gum. Wrigleys chewing gum came in packages of five sticks. That is the kind that most people bought. Their primary flavors were peppermint and spearmint. A pack of Wrigleys chewing gum cost five cents. Sometime during the depression, a new brand of chewing gum became available in the store. It was called Chum Gum. Chum Gum was also sold in packages of five sticks, but the price for a pack of chum gum was only one cent. The kids regularly purchased Chum Gum.

A pack of chum gum

During the Great Depression years in Sunnyside, there were several things that assisted the Mothers in maintaining their household chores. Early every morning, the milkman, who worked for the Shamokin Sanitary Milk Company, would deliver milk to the homes. There was a special receptacle on the front porch of the house, called the milkbox in which the milk would be placed. In those days, the milk was not homogenized and the cream floated to the top of the bottle. To make the milk homogenous, the bottle had to be well shaken before opening.

Great Depression era bottle
from the Shamokin Sanitary milk Company

About twice a week, the butcher would drive up to the households to sell his meat products. He would open a door at the back of his panel truck to display his products to the prospective buyer. The ladies would look over his products, make their choices and purchase the meat. The local farmer would come to the houses several days a week with his pickup truck loaded with fresh fruits and vegetables. This farmer, W. Edgar Erdman, also made and delivered scrapple, the best scrapple ever made. To those who do not know, scrapple is a special meat product made with cornmeal, pork, and who knows what else. It is boiled and comes in a loaf, and is sliced into thin pieces and fried. Scrapple not only tastes extremely good, but, if you eat it for breakfast, you will not get hungry again all day. Unfortunately, today it is impossible to find good scrapple. Apparently it is a lost art.

The foods of the depression era were fresh and had flavor. During the depression, for the meals, the vegetables were either fresh from the farm, or the garden, which tasted good, or from a can which were acceptable. Frozen vegetables, or other frozen foods, did not exist at that time. Today's frozen vegetables taste better than the commercially canned vegetables of the depression. The apples, during the depression, tasted better than today's apples, and they contained no chemicals, however they may contain several worm holes. Today, apples have a tough skin and less taste.

Meat came directly from the butcher and contained no steroids or other additives. The flavor of the meat was just as nature intended. Today, most meats are bland. Pork chops used to contain natural fat which made them very tasty, and they were fried in their natural fat. Today, pork chops, as sold in the grocery stores, have all of the fat cut from them, and are tasteless. To fry the pork chops, chemical fats are added to the frying pan. Lard is a natural food element and was used to fry eggs, meat and other foods. Food fried in lard has a good flavor. Today, food is contaminated with preservatives and other chemicals.

In the depression, sugar was used freely in the food. Today people use chemicals to sweeten their food or drinks.

The graham crackers of today have no resemblance to the graham crackers of the depression era. The depression graham crackers were thicker and had much more flavor. This is true of many of the popular prepared foods.

134

CHAPTER 6
POLITICS

In the election of 1936, Franklin Roosevelt defeated Governor Alf Landon of Kansas for president in a massive landslide election. Mr. McSherry, and his three sons, were cheering for Alf Landon to win. The kids would wear their candidate's pins to school. The Mount Union school kids had a majority of Landon backers.

When the stock market crashed in 1929, Herbert Hoover was the president of the United States, therefore he received all of the blame for the crash. Every president is always given credit for the good and given the blame for the bad while they are in office.

In 1932, Franklin Delano Roosevelt was elected to the presidency of the United States. He was a very popular president. In the early years of the Roosevelt presidency, Mr. & Mrs. Richard Chaundy became the parents of a new son. To honor the president, they named their new son Franklin Roosevelt Chaundy, however, the kids called the little boy "Fish".

All of the kids had nicknames at that time. Austin Chaundy was "Rat", Earl Chaundy was "chair", Robert Chaundy was "Dibbs", Wayne Taylor was "Gobbley the Gook", later shortened to "Gobbley", Wayne Knoebel was "Tony Cabutch the Barber's Son", later shortened to "Butch", Harry Harper was " Skinny Connect the Rainpipe", never shortened but later reverted to "Harry", Marlin Snyder was "Copper Sniffer Snyder", later shortened to "Snuffy", John Cook was simply "Cookie", and Jack Llewellyn was " Lucky". There were many more, but these serve as the gist of the nicknames.

Franklin Roosevelt was first elected as president in 1932 and he was reelected in 1936. The controversy started when he ran for reelection in 1940, because George Washington turned down a third term and every president after that followed that precedent. He was accused of trying to be a dictator. His excuse was that we should not change the government in the midst of the World War. He was elected to a third term. Then in 1944, he was elected to a fourth term. The war was still going on and he was a popular president, but many people were frightened because of his unprecedented long time in office. In 1945, he died in office and the vice president, Harry S. Truman, became president.

In 1933 Congress passed the National Recovery Act to give the President the authority to regulate industry in an attempt to raise prices to fight the depression. The concept of this was way over the head of the kids, but they noticed that most of the adults grumbled when they saw the insignia of that act posted on walls and in store windows. It meant that prices would go up, but wages would probably remain the same, thus increasing the hardships of the people.

There would be occasional baseball games played on a baseball field in Overlook. The field had three bases (rocks) placed in the proper locations, plus the home plate. The entire infield was reasonably level and raked to a rather smooth surface. A backstop screen was erected behind the catcher consisting of log posts with chicken wire attached. The outfield was irregular and contained weeds. These games were local kids, the older ones, against teams from other nearby areas. One of the players, the pitcher, was Earl Chaundy. Earl was better known as "chair', supposedly because he liked to sit. "Chair" was a great pitcher, striking out many of the opposition players. However, "Chair" did not do much fielding, only pitched. If a fly ball came close to him, he would walk over and catch it, but he never ran to catch a ball passing near him. Everyone liked "Chair" and appreciated him for his great pitching ability.

Another member of the Overlook team was Delmar Bailey. Delmar didn't always hit the ball when he was at bat, but he certainly had a mean swing. Delmar was the son of Mr. & Mrs. Elwood Bailey who had the farm directly behind the McSherry home. Delmar was in the Navy during World War Two. He was on board a destroyer in the battle of Okinawa, which was attacked by Japanese suicide planes known as kamakazies. The ship was hit by one diving plane, but fought on. They shot down several additional suicide planes, then they were hit again by another kamakazi. Badly damaged they continued to fight back. Finally they were hit by a third kamakazi whereby the ship rolled over on her side and sunk stern first into the ocean. Delmar Bailey went down with the ship, a major tragedy.

It should be noted that Bill McSherry was in that same battle with Delmar Bailey, but not on the same ship. Bill was on board a Battle Cruiser. Bill survived the war.

The political atmosphere, during the Great Depression, was probably pretty hot, but the kids in their Paradise did not pay much attention. The only way they did participate in the politics was during the local elections when people were running for all of the miscellaneous local offices. Each candidate would have a card printed showing the office they were running for, along with their party, probably their picture, and, of course, their name. All of these cards were the same size, and they were distributed generously throughout the neighborhood. The kids would collect as many of these cards as they could. Then the games started. Two or more kids, each having their handful of voting cards, commonly called "voties", would take turns laying down a card face up. When the last name of the politician of the last card laid down by the one person was topped by a card having a politician's name starting with the same letter, this player was the winner and would pick up the entire pile of cards.

Another card that the kids collected was picture cards of the mid-1930's Japanese attacks on China. These were found in packages of bubble gum which could be purchased at Kline's store in Sunnyside for one cent. The sheet of bubblegum was the same size as the card. These pictures were rather brutal. One example was a picture of planes bombing school busses resulting in fiery scenes.

CHAPTER 7
TRAVEL

Mr. McSherry always bought gas for his car at a gas station in Weight Scales, which was owned by Mr. Hoover who was a neighbor of the McSherrys in Sunnyside.   Mr. McSherry always bought five gallons of gas each time he went there. Five gallons cost one dollar.

In the mid-thirties, Mr. Hoover built several cabins on his land adjacent to the gas station. These cabins would be rented out to tourists for about one or two dollars a night. Cabins preceded motels.

When the driver wanted to purchase gas, he drove into the gas station and stopped alongside the pump. He stayed inside the car and opened his window. The attendant of the gas station would ask him how much gas he wanted, and upon receiving that information, he would pump the gas into the car's gas tank. After pumping the gas, the attendant would clean the car's windshield, then open the hood and check the oil level.   Upon doing this, he would collect from the driver the money for the gas.

Tires for cars during the Great Depression were not of the strength and quality that exist today. Whenever someone drove more than sixty miles, they could expect to have at least one flat tire.   People, in those days did not travel long distances very often, only for special occasions.

During the depression, in the State of Pennsylvania, the State would issue license plates for the cars. Every year each car got two plates, one for the front of the car and the other for the back of the car, and each year it was a different number. These plates were orange and blue. One year it would be blue numbers on an orange   background, and the next year it would be orange numbers on a blue background.

In that period of time, most people drove their cars at a speed of 35 to 40 miles per hour. 60 miles per hour was considered extremely fast and most people never drove that fast. People drove shorter distances than today. Most commuted only five to ten miles to their work. Cars had no seat belts. The cars were constructed with much heavier metal than today, therefore a collision did not do as much damage to the car as today's cars. However, the collapse of the superstructure of today's cars takes some of the impact out of the collision and, therefore, causes less injury to the passengers. Also, the cars of the depression had windows of glass, not safety glass. The person sitting in the front seat alongside the driver was in a precarious position. If there was a front-end collision, this person would be catapulted toward the front, his head would slam into the front windshield, breaking the windshield, and the person would be seriously cut by the glass on the head and neck. People named the seat alongside the driver as the sui-side seat.

Cars had no turn signals during the depression. If a driver was preparing to make a left turn, he opened his window and put his arm horizontally straight out. If he was planning a right turn, he opened the window and put his arm out of the window, bent his elbow and pointed straight upward.

The cars of the 1930's did not have power steering. A heavy car moving slowly required considerable energy to make a turn. In addition, the steering wheel did not automatically return to the neutral position when making a turn. Therefore, when completing a turn, the driver had to spin the wheel back to the neutral position.

In addition, the cars did not have heaters, so in the winter time, there were blankets in the car. Automatic transmissions did not exist until the year 1938, before that the clutch had to be pushed in to shift gears. The driver started in low gear, shifted into second gear, then into high gear, using the clutch each time. When stopped on an uphill area, the driver had to put his right foot on the brake and push the clutch in with his left foot. While in that situation, he had to shift the gears into low. To move the car up the hill, he had to remove his foot from the clutch, then to keep from drifting backwards down the hill, he had to rapidly move his foot from the brake pedal and hit the gas petal.

During the depression, the State Police watched over the traffic and issued tickets for offenses. They also chased and caught criminals. In the mid 1930's, they started driving cars that were totally white. The people called them the ghost cars. These troopers were generally very large and powerful looking. At least that's what it appeared to a little kid. They were extremely polite, but firm. The people respected their state troopers.

Mr. McSherry's 1936 Lafayette

Calvin Burrell's 1938 Plymouth

CHAPTER 8
NEWS

During the Great Depression, there were many major news items being written in the newspapers, and broadcast on the radio. The people in the neighborhood would discuss these news items. That is how most of the news met the ears of the kids.

In Sunnyside, the Shamokin newspaper, entitled the "Shamokin News Dispatch" was faithfully delivered every day, except Sunday, by Austin Chaundy, who was a neighbor of the McSherry family. Austin delivered these newspapers for years beginning when he was probably about twelve years old. The only thing that the McSherry boys read in the newspaper was the comics. Such as Alley Oop, Joe Palooka, Maggie and Jiggs, Dick Tracy, among others. Sadly, Austin Chaundy was killed in France in 1944 while serving wih a tank division in the United States Army during World War 2.

Austin Chaundy
1923-1944

On March 1, 1932, the 20 month old son of aviation hero, Charles Lindbergh, was kidnapped from his second floor bedroom in the home of Mr. & Mrs. Lindbergh in Hopewell, New Jersey. Because of the Lindbergh fame, the news swept across the United States. The horror of the kidnapping was discussed everywhere.

The kidnapper gained access to the child's bedroom by climbing a ladder to an open window of the bedroom. As a result of this kidnapping, and all of the publicity and discussions, young Jack, who was four years old, was frightened for several days, thinking that a kidnapper would climb up a ladder to his bedroom window and kidnap him. His Mother reassured him, many times, that he was safe, and that he would not be kidnapped. It took Jack some time before he calmed down and forgot the whole episode.

On May 28, 1934, the Dionne quintuplets were born near Callander, Ontario, Canada. They were the first identical quintuplets known to survive their infancy. They were five identical girls. Unfortunately, due to their unusual status, they lived an unfortunate childhood confined to a commercial style of life being on display to the public as an oddity.

EMILIE   YVONNE   CECILE   ANNETTE   MARIE
1937

A big news item occurred on July 22, 1934. John Dillinger, a notorious bank robber who was number one on the Government's most wanted criminals list, was shot and killed by Government agents, at the age of 31, as he came out of a movie theatre in Chicago. Because of his notoriety, this created much conversation between the people at that time. Because of all of the excitement, young Jack, who was six years old at the time, remembers it well.

In 1935, under the leadership of Benito Mussolini, Italy invaded the African nation of Ethiopia. The Emperor of Ethiopia, Haile Selassie, resisted as well as he could, but the Ethiopian capital of Addis Ababa fell in 1936. Haile Selassie successfully escaped and was honored by most of the world. On the following Christmas, many of the children of Sunnyside, who collected and played with toy soldiers, found toy Ethiopian soldiers under the Christmas tree.

On Sunday, October 30, 1938, actor Orson Welles narrated a halloween radio show entitled The War of the Worlds" for the Series, "The Mercury Theatre on the Air". The show was narrated in the first person like a news cast. It described how the Martians were invading New Jersey in great detail. People who tuned in late, and not knowing that it was just a show, took it seriously. It created quite a stir and some panic. Young Jack remembers that the next day many people in the neighborhood were very excited about it, and were discussing and debating it. Some thought Orson Welles should be arrested, others laughed it off.

On May 6, 1937, a terrible disaster occurred at Lakehurst, New Jersey. This made the news and was discussed by people everywhere. As the German passenger airship, Hindenburg, was attempting to moor to a landing mast, it suddenly caught fire and was destroyed. There were 97 people on board the airship, 35 of these people were killed, and one person on the ground was killed. It is quite amazing that anyone survived. This incident was not soon forgotten, and because of its horror, the passenger airship business was forever ended.   Children heard all the details, but fortunately, children have the ability to quickly let such things pass into history.

The airship Hindenberg exploding

CHAPTER 9
THE SUMMER OF 1937
A TOUR BY AUTOMOBILE ACROSS THE UNITED STATES

Right in the middle of the Great Depression, the McSherry Family purchased a new car, and went on an unbelievable three month automobile tour of practically the entire United States! How could they do that?

In the year 1937, Mr. McSherry retired from the United States Navy having served sixteen years of active duty and fourteen years in the fleet reserve. He apparently received a bonus sum of money for his retirement, because he traded in his 1930 Graham and purchased a 1936 Lafayette. He then planned a cross-country trip, for the family, to California to visit his brother, Raymond, who lived in Mendocino County in Northern California.

The Lafayette was an unusual car, but that's why Mr. McSherry purchased it. It was a sedan with a full width front seat and a full width back seat. Three people could sit on the front seat with the person in the center straddling the floor mounted gear shift lever. The back seat provided clear sitting for three people. The most unusual feature in the car was that the backrest of the back seat was hinged at the top and could be rotated upward exposing the total trunk area. The object for this was to provide travelers a comfortable bed in the car. To do this, the hinged backrest was raised upward and propped in that position with two short posts which rested on the armrests of the back seat. The three seat unit from the front was removed and placed over the floor area in the front of the back seat. The backrest of the front seat was moved forward to provide the necessary room to place the seat cushion into its position. When this was done, the tops of the two side by side cushions were on the same level. The bed was now prepared and ready. Three people could lay side by side in that bed with their heads at the back of the front seat backrest, and their feet extending into the trunk area. He bought this car, with the bed, because he was planning a long car trip and figured the bed could be helpful if necessary.

The trip was well planned. At that time gas stations always had maps which they would give to their customers. But Mr. McSherry, better known as Dad, went further than that. He knew where he wanted to go, but he needed maps to determine which highways he wanted to use. He met with a representative of the Conoco Oil Company. They discussed his plans and the representative prepared a bound album-like atlas of road maps. On these maps, the proposed route of the entire trip was highlighted with a yellow line. Dad laid this map album alongside his seat and it was always there to guide him as he progressed on the trip. Basically, the trip was planned to go west via the southern states, then go north through California, Oregon, and Washington. The return trip was across the northern states and back to Pennsylvania.

On June 2, 1937, with the car totally loaded with everything that was needed, they left Sunnyside and headed west. Uncle Calvin, Mom's brother, was given the responsibility of looking after the house while they were gone. Dad had two leather satchels which probably contained changes of clothes for the entire family. The seating arrangement in the car was most likely conceived by Mom. Dad, of course, did all of the driving. Mom sat on the front seat alongside Dad. Bill, who was the oldest, sat on the right side of the back seat behind Mom. Dave sat on the left side of the back seat. Jack, being the youngest, was assigned to sit in the middle of the back seat, apparently so that he could not hang out of the window and probably fall out of the car. Dave and Bill each had a window alongside them where they could see everything. Being in the middle, Jack had no window alongside him, but he could see quite well straight ahead through the windshield. This seating arrangement never changed during the trip.

When they went on this trip, it must be remembered that Jack was only nine years old, and probably did not pay too much attention to important things. He did notice many things that interested his child mind.

They drove Southwest from Sunnyside toward the western end of the Maryland-Pennsylvania border. There they crossed into Maryland and into West Virginia. They usually drove between 200 and 250 miles each day, so that means they most likely stayed overnight somewhere in western Pennsylvania. In 1937, there were no motels. Travelers in those days would stay in tourist cabins. These tourist cabins were constructed by individuals as an investment for the tourist trade. Perhaps the owner of a gas station would own several acres of land adjacent to his gas station and built four or five individual cabins on that land to rent to the travelers. These cabins were few and far between, and you could never plan ahead to locate one. When you found some cabins, and it was getting late in the day, it was prudent to stop for the night. Rent for one cabin was usually about $ 2.00 for the night.

At the beginning of the trip, everything was about the same as Pennsylvania. There were no expressways at that time. All of the roads were two lanes. Most of the main roads were paved with applications of crushed stone and hot tar. Many of the secondary roads were not paved. In those days, traffic was very light. Not everyone had a car and most people did not do a lot of traveling. The further west they went, the less traffic there was. Often they were the only car on the road. They passed through the southern tip of Ohio and on into Indiana. The first things that they noticed were, when they got out to the flatlands of Indiana and Illinois, were the long, straight, flat roads. While driving across those States on a straight, level concrete highway, mother pointed out to the kids that there was water on the road up ahead. It could be seen very clearly from a distance, but when they got to it, there was no water there. It was a mirage. These were common as they continued westward.

From Illinois, they crossed over the Mississippi River into Missouri. That was exciting to Jack because he knew all about the Mississippi because of his Geography classes in school. In Missouri, they stopped at a cabin early in the evening, so Bill, Dave and Jack were running around the area having a good time. About that time, the Owner of the cabins hollered at them, primarily Jack, and told them to stay out of a certain area where they were climbing around on piles of old lumber. This annoyed Jack, so he got even with him by turning the water on at an outside faucet. The next morning when they were leaving, he looked for the faucet and it was still running with water. He was happy and pleased.

Missouri

They continued westward in Missouri. They saw a sign alongside the road that read "worms for sale". They thought that was very funny and unusual, so they stopped and took pictures of it. At that point Mom got some sandwiches out of the car and they had lunch. They mostly ate snacks and sandwiches as they traveled. Occasionally they stopped at a Café for lunch. It was on this trip that Jack was introduced to the word "café". When he read it on the signs, he pronounced it caff. Of course he was laughed at for that, so he finally learned the correct pronunciation. Missouri was the last state, in going west, that was basically green with trees and grass. Then they passed into Oklahoma where the grasses were brownish and the trees were fewer.

Claremore, Oklahoma

They stayed overnight in a cabin in Claremore, Oklahoma. Claremore was the home town of Will Rogers, one of Dad's heroes. He apparently scheduled to go through that town on purpose because of Will Rogers. One of the highlights of that town was comic books. In the morning, Bill and Dave took a walk down the street, and when they came back, they each had a comic book. The McSherry kids never saw a comic book before. The only comics they ever saw were in the newspapers. When Jack saw this, he went to the same store and bought a comic book for ten cents. It was all stories about Dick Tracy. Apparently that was the time when comic books first hit the market.

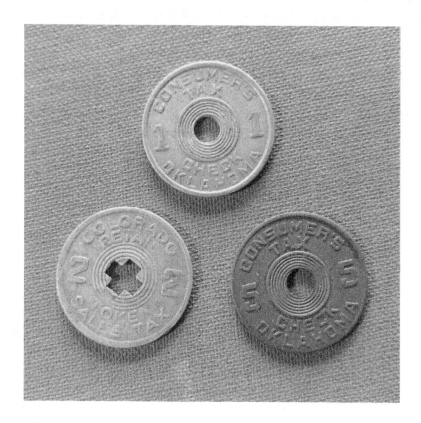

In Oklahoma, and again in Colorado, the McSherrys received strange coins in their change when they purchased something. These coins were tax tokens, some being one mil in value and others being 5 mils in value. Ten mils equaled one cent. The above photo shows these coins.

They continued westward through Oklahoma. Soon they passed through an area where there were oil wells all over the fields on both sides of the road. Pumps were operating on all of the wells. Oklahoma is a very flat state, and the roads were mostly unpaved.

Then they entered Texas. They traveled through Texas for quite a few days. It is a big state. It was in Texas that they first saw cactus. It was the close to the ground, prickly kind. They parked the car and walked around in the desert-like soil and tried not to step on the cactus. Dad dug up several cactus plants, along with the roots and some of the surrounding soil, and put them into some tin cans. His idea was to take them home and plant them in Pennsylvania. Because they were soon going to cross the border into Mexico and back, he put the potted cacti under the hood with the engine of the car so that the officials at the border would not find them and take them from him.

The open range In Texas

As they drove on, they saw a very large jackrabbit running across the sandy ground. Before long they also saw several armadillos walking along the road. They eventually arrived in El Paso near the western line of Texas, and on the border to Mexico. They drove across the border into Mexico. They drove several miles on a dirt road through an area that was mostly uninhabited. Then they came to some Mexican houses alongside the road. They were crude houses with thatched roofs. They stopped at one of them and Dad took some pictures. There were children outside playing, they appeared to be curious about the Americans, but also afraid. The McSherrys did not linger, but got back in the car and drove a little further. They went to the town of Juarez where they walked around in the streets for a while. After a short excursion in Mexico, they turned around and returned to El Paso. When they crossed the border into and out of Mexico, no one found the cacti under the hood. All was well, except when Dad finally got to check on his cactus, they were all dead. Apparently the heat of the engine was too much for them. Before they left Texas, Dad and Mom bought Bill, Dave, and Jack each an authentic cowboy hat.

Texas

The road from El Paso to Carlesbad

Leaving Texas, they entered New Mexico. One of their stops was the famous Carlsbad Caverns.

The entrance into the Carlsbad Caverns

They walked down a long ramp to get to the entrance to the caverns. The front opening to the caverns was huge. It seemed to cover half of the hill in which it existed. Along with a group of other people, they entered the caverns being led by a guide who gave them information about the caverns, and described the items at which they were looking. Of course there were the conventional stalactites and stalagmites. They followed a path through the caverns, walking through very large areas with stalactites and stalagmites within touch, but with additional stalactites and stalagmites behind them and more behind those, stretching out over a very wide area on both sides of the path. In many areas the ceiling of the cavern was very high, and in other areas the ceiling was just above their heads. They walked uphill and downhill as they progressed through the caverns. There were large bodies of water on the floor adjacent to the path in several locations. The guide told them that the caverns extended underground for a distance of five miles. They did not walk that far, but to Jack, it seemed to be a long distance. After their long hike, they entered into a very large area with a very high ceiling. The guide called it their ballroom. There everyone mingled and discussed the caverns. There were people there from all across the United States, and probably from many other countries. One old lady took a liking to Jack and gave him an orange. An elevator returned them to the ground surface above. When they arrived on the surface of the ground, it was dusk. Dad knew that the caverns were inhabited with bats and these bats came out of the caverns when it started to get dark and fly around the area. So they waited, and soon the sky was full of bats flying around overhead. They returned to their car and were on their way west.

They entered into Arizona on unpaved roads. In Arizona there were some very large cacti. The ones with the arms that can be seen in the western movies. Dad parked the car, and Mom, Bill, Dave, and Jack posed in front of one very large cacti and Dad took their picture with his box camera. The deserts of Arizona and the large cactus were totally different than the green woods and lawns back in Pennsylvania. There were Indians sitting along the side of the road as they drove by.

Cactus in Arizona

They crossed Arizona near the northern end of the state and stayed for the night in a cabin at the border with Nevada. The new Boulder dam was visible from their cabin. The name of the dam was later changed to Hoover Dam. Construction for the dam began in 1931 and it was completed in 1936, just about a year before the McSherrys got there. It was a large concrete structure hanging between two mountains. There were also Indian teepees near the cabin.

They crossed the Arizona-Nevada border and headed southwest through the southern tip of Nevada, then crossed into California and headed for the area around San Diego.

On the road again, they went into Los Angeles, Hollywood, and Beverly Hills. They stayed overnight in Tarzana, California. The next day they got on a small steamer, possibly about 40 feet long, and took a 30-mile cruise to Santa Catalina Island. That was an exciting thing to do, especially for Dad who was retired from the Navy. The sailing vessel rolled along in the waves heading toward

Catalina Island. Mom and Jack both got somewhat seasick, especially Jack. However they made it to Santa Catalina, looked around on the island, then came back to the mainland.

On Board the Steamer, Avalon, headed for Catalina Island.
Jack's face shows signs of seasickness

They found cabins in that area, in a village called Thousand Oaks and stayed there for the night. The next morning, when they awoke, they heard the roar of lions. Bill and Dave went to investigate. Jack stayed in the cabin where it was safe. They came back with the information that there was a place near their cabin where someone was making a movie. So, all five of the McSherrys went to see this. When they got there, they found that a movie was being made with Frank Buck. Frank Buck was famous at that time for catching wild animals and bringing them back alive for zoos and circuses. The movie set consisted of an area possibly 100 feet square. The area was filled with cut trees and underbrush, propped up so they looked like they were growing. In effect, they created a jungle. In that jungle, hidden behind some underbrush, was a wooden cage. The employee who was there explained that there would be a leopard in the cage when they were filming, and at the right time he would be released to run out after some human. This was all part of the scheduling for the filming of the movie.

Travelling on, they came to an old Mission, called the Santa Barbara Mission, which was built in the late 1700's by the Spanish Catholic Priests. They stopped, parked the car, and went into the Mission. Even to Jack it was historic and very interesting.

The Santa Barbara Mission

The Orange Tree

They left Thousand Oaks and headed North in California. Somewhere along the way, they went through some orange orchards. Dad stopped the car alongside an orange tree loaded with ripe oranges. He had Mom and the kids stand alongside the tree for a picture, which they did. Dad took the picture. Then Mom reached up into the tree and picked herself an orange. Seeing that, Bill, Dave and Jack did the same. Then Mom reached into the tree again and got one for Dad. They then got back into the car, drove off, and ate the sweetest oranges that they ever tasted.

From Thousand Oaks to San Francisco is about 400 miles, so it apparently took several days to travel that distance. When they got to the San Francisco area, they came to the Oakland Bay Bridge which they crossed to get into San Francisco. They walked the streets of San Francisco, and past a Chinese restaurant which had a large window display of some of their foods. There were many food items in that display which Jack would not have touched with a ten foot pole. But the one item that really upset him was a pan full of blood pudding.

Looking at the bay in San Francisco was exciting. Dad probably enjoyed it even more than the rest of the family because he was with the Navy's Great White Fleet when it stopped there during the fleet's famous cruise around the world from 1907 to 1909.

The Golden Gate Bridge in San Francisco
1937

Leaving San Francisco, and heading north, they crossed the Golden Gate Bridge over the Bay. The construction of the bridge had just been completed and opened to public traffic about a week before they crossed it. They continued northward on Route 101. The shoreline became rockier and more mountainous as they traveled northward. The road was a two lane, curvy road made of crushed stone and hot tar. The scenery got more interesting the further north they traveled. Eventually they arrived in the town of Willets. They knew they were getting close to the home of Uncle Raymond and Aunt Nina because their home was only fifty miles north of Willets. They continued on their way, around curves through the mountainous and tree covered areas. Finally, on the right side of the road just after going around a sharp curve, there was a driveway that went back to Uncle Raymond's house. They had arrived. The drive from Pennsylvania to Uncle Raymond's house took about two weeks. They arrived at Uncle Raymond's house on June 18.

Uncle Raymond's house was located several hundred feet from the road. It was a single story house. He referred to it as a bungalow. Inside there was a dining room, sitting room, small kitchen, bathroom, and two bedrooms. Jack doesn't recall ever going out the front door, but he supposed there was one. At the front of the house there was a wooden porch across the entire front of the house. The back door went out from the kitchen onto a small wooden stoop. One step down and you were in his back yard. In his back yard, he had a garden and quite a few peach trees. His property was surrounded by a wire fence, primarily to keep the deer out. Beyond the fence, the land extended back several hundred feet to the base of the mountain, where it was covered with trees and sloped steeply upward.

His kitchen stove served to heat the house as well as to prepare food. The nights there were fairly cold considering that they were there during the summer. The kitchen stove didn't do much to resist that cold during the night. Uncle Raymond burned redwood in his stove. He had large diameter cross-sections of short pieces of redwood logs. He would set these pieces in the right position, then swing an axe to split them into narrow planks. They split uniformly and straight to form pieces about four inches wide, one-half inch thick and possibly eighteen inches long. These pieces fit well into his stove. The redwood split perfectly because the wood was dry and the grain was absolutely straight. After watching Uncle Raymond split the wood, Jack decided that he would help him. He got the axe, lined up the log, and successfully split nice pieces of the wood. While there, he split a large amount of firewood, and enjoyed every minute of it.

On the evening of June 22, Uncle Raymond, Dad, and the three boys went to the neighbor's house and sat on the front porch to listen to a boxing bout on the radio. It was between Joe Louis, the challenger, and Jim Braddock, the champion. Joe Louis knocked Braddock out in the 8th round and became the boxing champion of the world.

Uncle Raymond had a chow dog which ran loose in the yard. When Jack went outside, if the dog was around, he would chase Jack. While he was chasing Jack, he would slobber, and Jack ran as fast as he could around the house to get away from him. Fortunately, the dog got tired quickly and stopped the chase. Jack did not like that dog.

Across the highway from Uncle Raymond's house was a path, wide enough for a car, which sloped down to the Eel River. The river may have been about 30 feet wide. It had some deep spots that were adequate for swimming. Dad, Mom, Bill, Dave, Uncle Raymond, Aunt Nina, and Jack went down there to swim almost every day. A neighbor girl, Violet Rhea, 12 years old, also would join them. The water was cold, so Jack preferred sitting in a stagnate pool alongside the river because the water was much warmer in there. The only ones that could swim were Dad, Uncle Raymond, Aunt Nina and Violet. While there, with a lot of effort and practice, Bill and Dave both learned to swim doggie paddle. Jack did not learn to swim because he didn't try and he spent most of his time sitting in the stagnate pool.

Jack went fishing in Mendoceno County
California

Whenever they went to the River, they would see many snakes. They were water snakes, mostly about eight to twelve inches long, but some were much bigger. They would swim in the water too. The river also had fish in it. They were trout and all of them were about six inches long. Uncle Raymond made each of the boys a fishpole. He cut down small trees and put a string and fish-hook on them. He gave them fish eggs to use as bait. Bill and Dave each caught several fish. Jack caught one fish, about 6-inches long, and pulled it out of the water. Then with the fish still on the hook, he ran all the way up the trail and across the road to Uncle Raymond's house to show it to everyone. Uncle Raymond took it off the hook, and cleaned it. He fried it for Jack for supper. The way they ate those trout was interesting. They fried them with the head and tail still on them, then to eat them, they would hold the head in one hand and the tail in the other and eat them off the bone the same way that you would eat the corn off of a cob. When the fish was eaten, all that remained was the skeleton of a fish with the head on one end and the tail on the other. Those fried fish were very tasty. That was the first fish that Jack ever caught. It was also the only one that he ever caught. Occasionally while they were there, Uncle Raymond would go fishing and bring back enough fish for everyone for supper.

Swimming in the Eel River

Rafting on the Eel River

By way of a dirt road, the Pacific Ocean was about seven miles from Uncle Raymond's house. They drove over to the ocean walked around on the sandy beach. However, the beach was not like Atlantic City. The sand was gray, and fairly soft so that it was difficult to walk on it. Throughout the beach there were huge gray rocks. The shoreline behind the beach contained rocky cliffs. The beach width from the cliffs to the ocean was probably less than one-hundred feet. They did not swim in the ocean.

The Jack McSherry family and the Raymond McSherry family
at the Coolidge Tree

Several miles north of Uncle Raymond's house were forests of redwood trees. These trees were huge. Some were 10 to 12 feet in diameter and 300 feet high. They were hundreds of years old. There was a side road that passed through a carved out redwood tree. Dad drove the car on that road and through the tree. There was also a gift shop inside the base of a hollowed out redwood tree.

On one occasion, Uncle Raymond and Aunt Nina drove the group to Willets, California to see a Rodeo. There was the arena where the action took place, and the visitors sat in wooden bleachers to watch. There were cowboys riding bucking broncos, and bucking steers. There were also cowboys riding horses and roping cattle. There were cowboys competing in all kinds of western demonstrations. This was truly an authentic cowboy rodeo. It went on for hours and was entertaining and exciting for the entire time.

On several occasions, Uncle Raymond, Dad, Bill, Dave, and Jack took hikes up into the mountain behind the house. It was steep and rugged. They would see deer and other animals up there. Uncle Raymond was an outdoorsman. He lived off the land. When they bought groceries, they had to drive north to the nearest town, Garberville, which was a one-way trip of 25 miles.

The McSherrys stayed with Uncle Raymond for about a month. On August 10 they said "goodbye" and headed north on Route 101. The road was parallel to the coastline and the ocean could be seen most of the way along that route. The area was mountainous, full of trees, and the shoreline contained rocky cliffs. The road was paved with crushed stone and tar, and it contained continuous curves. After driving several hours, they passed through Eureka, California. They were now about 100 miles from the Oregon border.

In several hours, they crossed the line into Oregon. There was not anything particularly interesting in Oregon except the beautiful scenery along the ocean. They followed the coast line. Most of the roadside areas were covered with trees. They eventually crossed the line into Washington State and went to the city of Bremerton, Washington where Dad went to see the Mayor. The Mayor of Bremerton, at that time, was a Navy friend of Dad's. The entire family met the mayor. They left Bremerton and went over to Seattle. The next day after leaving Seattle, they headed eastward. They went to see the Grand Coulee Dam which was under construction. The Dam is located about 90 miles northwest of Spokane. Construction started in 1933 and was completed in 1941. The dam is a concrete structure and is three times as large as the Hoover Dam.

Grand Coulee Dam under Construction

They crossed the border from Washington into Idaho. Then headed southeast through Idaho skirting past the southern border of Montana, and eastward into Wyoming. There, in the northwest corner of Wyoming, they entered into Yellowstone National Park. Yellowstone National Park is like no other place in the United States. As soon as they entered the park, they saw black bears alongside the highway. The bears actually walked up to the car, stood on their hind feet, looked in the window of the car looking for a food handout. The McSherrys accommodated them by giving them marshmallows. There were many bears alongside the road in the park. In other areas there were deer and other small animals. The entire park was in its natural condition. Then they came to the geysers. There were all kinds of geysers. One of the most famous and largest was the Old Faithful Geyser. This geyser got its name because it erupted precisely every hour. When it erupted, it blew steam and water possibly 40 feet into the air. They stood there and watched that geyser quite a while, several times. There were mud flats where the mud was churning and boiling. They walked across one of those on a wooden pedestrian bridge. Yellowstone National Park was interesting and fascinating. It was one of the highlights of the trip.

Bears in Yellowstone getting some marshmallows
From the McSherrys

Great Fountain Geyser
Yellowstone Park

When they left Yellowstone, they headed east, just south of the Montana border. Wyoming was cowboy country. They would see them riding along on horseback in the fields adjacent to the road tending to their cattle. A short distance east of Yellowstone, they drove through the town of Cody. There was a lake there called the Buffalo Bill Lake. The area around the lake consisted of very high rocky hills. They drove through a long tunnel, which was cut through the rock, alongside the lake. About 170 miles east of Yellowstone, they turned northward and crossed the line into Montana. They continued northward, driving through the Crow Indian Reservation and to the Custer Battlefield at the Little Bighorn River. This is where the Sioux Indians completely annihilated General George Custer and his United States Cavalry troops. Custer attacked the Indians with some 100 troops. There were 3000 Sioux Indians. The site was a large field, with no trees, but with knee-high yellow grass. There was one large granite stone To commemorate what happened.

Most people are unaware that cactus grows in Montana. While in that state, they saw many   cacti, the kind that is low to the ground and has flat, oval leaves. This is the same type of cactus that grows in Texas and New Mexico and other south-western states, the kind that Dad potted in Texas. Dad dug up three of these plants, including the roots and surrounding soil, and put them in tin cans. This time he put the cactus in the trunk of the car for the trip home. When they got back to Sunnyside, Dad planted the plants in the back yard and they not only survived, but they continued to grow. In 1939, when the McSherrys moved to Tharptown, they took the cacti along and planted them in the ground in the back yard adjacent to the fence between their property and that of their neighbor, Rachel Miller. The cactus continued to grow. However, apparently because the moisture in Pennsylvania is much greater than in Montana, the lower part of the cactus would rot away, but new shoots would grow out of the top. In that manner, the cactus flourished. Apparently, when Dad and Mom moved to Camp Hill, Pennsylvania, they dug up the cacti and took them along. The cactus grew in the back yard of Dad & Mom's home at 101 N. 24th Street in Camp Hill.

Mount Rushmore Memorial under Construction   1937
South Dakota

They went back down into Wyoming and continued eastward, and crossed the line into South Dakota. As soon as they crossed into South Dakota, they were in the Black Hills. A short distance inside South Dakota, and in the Black Hills, is the Mount Rushmore National Monument. When they arrived there, they parked in a small crushed stone parking lot. There were no buildings. They looked across the valley toward the mountain and there were the faces of some of the Presidents of the United States carved into the rocky side of the mountain. At that time, the faces of Washington and Jefferson were completed. The upper half of Lincoln's face was finished, but they were still carving the lower half. They had not started carving Theodore Roosevelt's face. This was an impressive sight. The men carving the faces were on some scaffolding. Others were sitting on small boards hanging at the end of a rope. The men looked like flies on George Washington's nose. They stayed and looked at that fascinating work of art for quite a while. Then they got back in the car and headed east.

Leaving Mount Rushmore, they traveled only a short distance and arrived in the Bad Lands of South Dakota. This area consisted of dunes strewn irregularly across the land. The dunes had very high peaks and were generally round. This pattern of dunes extended southward about 90 miles to the border between South Dakota and Nebraska. This was, in effect, a hilly desert, extremely dry, with no water anywhere and with no vegetation. One dune looked like the other. It was said that if any person ventured into that area, he would become hopelessly lost and would never return. It was also said that criminals would be turned loose there only to become lost and succumb to the elements. The observation of this unusual and formidable sight was an adventure in itself.

The Badlands, South Dakota

A highway tunnel through the badlands

More Badlands

Leaving the badlands, they headed east and crossed the line into Minnesota and across Wisconsin and into the upper peninsula of Michigan. They then passed into the province of Ontario, Canada. Their destination was Callander, Ontario, which is about 175 miles north of Toronto. They went there to see the Dionne quintuplets, who, at that time were three years old. The Dionne quintuplets were five identical girls born to Mr. & Mrs. Dionne. In those days, these girls were of world-wide interest because identical quintuplets were extremely rare. Because they were so rare, and they were born to a rather poor family, somehow Doctor Dafoe, who delivered them, either took custody, or was given custody of them. A special building was constructed to house them and to take care of them. This building was also constructed so that tourists could observe them as they played in an enclosed play yard. The McSherrys paid admission and walked through a structure which had windows to look into the play yard. They watched the little girls as they played. They were told that the girls could not see them because there were screens on the windows. There was also a souvenir shop where they bought some post cards containing pictures of the girls. Looking back on it, the girls would have been better off living with their parents.

The Home of the Dionne Family where the quintuplets were born
Callander, Ontario

Leaving Callander, they headed south through Ontario, then turned east and went into Buffalo, New York. They then traveled southward across the western end of New York State, and entered into Pennsylvania. With another days drive, they arrived home in Sunnyside. They arrived in Sunnyside on the 28th of August. During the entire trip, they had no flat tires or other car troubles.

Based on measurements on maps, it is estimated that the entire trip consisted of about 7000 miles. They had completed a journey that most people never have the opportunity to experience, or could ever dream of experiencing, and this was accomplished during the Great Depression.

THAT IS THE WAY IT WAS LIVING IN THE GREAT DEPRESSION. PARENTS HAD A TOUGH TIME, BUT THE KIDS LIVED IN PARADISE.

The following is a biography of the author
of
"PARADISE IN SUNNYSIDE, LIFE IN THE GREAT DEPRESSION"

THE LIFE OF JACK L. McSHERRY, Jr.

Author Anonymous

******

CHAPTER I

"Ah, everyone!" proclaimed Greenebaum - twas just as McSherry was proceeding with responses to blundering bureauocracy - several young men who were meeting with the great Greenebaum had the honor to be introduced to him. Scarcely were they past the customary greetings when Greenebaum asked eagerly, "How fares your friend and dauntless comrade, the great McSherry?" "He is very well", replied the youths, brightening at the thought that they were the comrades of McSherry; - Ah, gentlemen!" rejoined Greenebaum, "McSherry can never be otherwise than well, - The extent of his fame is full, - Future generations will talk of him with reverence as the originator of the maxims of a job well done; "I want it done now!, I want it done right!, and I want it done my way!"

Who, then, that has a glimmer of respect for those who have preceded them, and who wish to maintain the accuracy of History, and must wish to know the History of him whose name could even awaken a sigh from Greenebaum?

Though, isn't his History already known? Haven't the Bureaucrats already spread his name among society? Hasn't the gleam of his life already lighted the streams and hillsides of his community? Lo! he has lighted the sewers and cesspools of all areas of his neighborhood.

But this is not half of his fame. True, he has been seen in greatness, but it is only in the stories which I have yet to tell which

181

will glorify his name and character unto the glory and gold that he truly deserves. These stories are not of his public greatness and outspoken heroism, indeed they are of his private life, a life veiled from the public awareness. Behind this curtain of private life, where the millions have not cast eyes upon him, this is where the true mettle of a man is measured. His actions were not for the benefit of the public, and serve no motive for self promotion. Indeed, his private life and actions reflect the true greatness of the man! It is to these actions which the youth of today should pay attention, for every youth may someday become a McSherry - A McSherry in wisdom and modesty - in energy and honor - and consequently a McSherry, in what alone deserves the name UNIVERSAL AWE and ADMIRATION.

CHAPTER II
BIRTH AND EDUCATION

"Children like the babes of a cow,
As they are form'd forever grow."

To this day, numbers of people cannot find the faith to believe that Jack McSherry was born a middle-class common person in the rural area of Pennsylvania. "He is surely a descendent of European Monarchy; So great a person could not have been born in rural Pennsylvania."

Absurd! Why that's the ultimate of reasons why he should have been born in rural Pennsylvania. The strength beheld of hardworking, diligent, honorable, working people of this area would certainly serve as the bosom of wisdom and modesty for the arrival and rearing of this great person unto the world!

Accordingly, we find Pennsylvania the honored cradle of McSherry, who was born in Shamokin, Northumberland County, Pennsylvania, the 14th day of March, 1928. His father, whose name was James Jackson Lawrence McSherry, later reduced in all modesty to Jack L. McSherry, was also a Pennsylvanian as was his father before him.

Jack's father, having served his nation for many years in the United States Navy, arrived in a small hamlet called Bear Gap, also situated in the County of Northumberland, seeking work on a project for the construction of a dam.

Our hero's father must have possessed either a very pleasing person, or highly polished manners, or perhaps both; for, from what I can learn, he was at the time nearly 38 years old! For upon his arrival in Bear Gap, he met Ivy Burrell, who, on the other hand, was universally toasted as the belle of Bear Gap, and was in the full bloom and freshness of the love-inspiring age of twenty-five.

This meeting resulted in a short courtship, followed by the marriage of Jack L. McSherry and Ivy Burrell.

By this marriage, Mr. McSherry had three sons - William, David, and Jack, Jr.

Before Jack, Jr. was born, but after the birth of William and David, Mr. McSherry moved his family from Bear Gap to a small hamlet called "Sunnyside", located about three miles north of Shamokin, Pennsylvania. It was here that the family lived when Jack, Jr. was born. This house in which little Jack lived is still to be seen.

The first place of education to which little Jack was ever sent, was a four-roomed, brick schoolhouse called "Mount Union School" located in the village of Overlook. Miss Jemima Eltringham was his first teacher, having first taught him the knowledge of letters! Young Jack was early sent to school. At the young age of five, he trudged daily the one-half mile to the school, diligent and determined, as he fought the snows, the winds, rain, and at times, the heat of Hades.

In school, Jack was a determined student. He participated in the learning process, and was ever mindful of the teacher's explanation. Notwithstanding, certain detractions from the standard events of the learning day, did enter into Jack's educational process. It seems, on one occasion, young Jack was deep in thought on matters of great importance, when he chewed the eraser from the top of his wooden pencil, thus leaving the twisted metal casement of the eraser at the end of the pencil. While contemplating his future greatness, young Jack proceeded to rotate the metal tip of the pencil onto the top of his brand new desk, thereby making scratches of a great multitude onto the entire top surface of the desk.

Much to her consternation, upon observation of young Jack's scratching procedure, Miss Eltringham became much distraught, and left the room in search of Miss Pensyl, the principal of the school. Upon finding Miss Pensyl, both ladies returned to the classroom and stood over young Jack, as he sat at his desk, and excitedly discussed the resultant scratches. After some discussion and observation, they brought a bottle of liquid from which they applied with a soft cloth the liquid upon the entire surface of the desk. In Jack's opinion, the surface looked much better, and the scratches were less pronounced. However, the teachers concluded that the desk did not look good, and proceeded to tie our hero's hands together behind his back, and made him stand in the corner at the front of the classroom. Jack's instructions were to face the corner, but in all of his wisdom and determination, chose to face the class instead, however, with a look of distaste to transmit his feelings of inequity to the class. After some time, Jack was able to release his bindings, and the classmates knowing that he was truly a great person, assumed that he had cut the bindings with his trusty knife which he carried in the pocket of his high-top shoe.

But, though Jack was sent early to school, yet he learned the sensibilities of life, and the foundations to his greatness from the example of his compassionate Father, and from the determinations and teachings of his patient Mother.

Little Jack's father was a man who knew no prejudices, a man without vindictiveness, and a man without enemy. It was by these virtues of his father that little Jack learned that all men are, first, men, and nothing other. Association with others was based on nothing other than the goodness or corruptness of the individual person.

Jack's patient Mother would extoll the virtues of self-determination, and warn against the evils of life. Thus nurtured by his wise mother, Jack learned to make his own decisions, thinking for himself, nay, not listening to foolish ideas or goading of others. Greatness in the man was formed within the mind of a child by the lessons and examples of those who cared.

The following anecdote is a case in point. It is too exemplary to be lost, and too true to be doubted. It was told to me by an old man who lived near a distant cousin who never met McSherry, but who heard of him. I am indebted to this old man for this great truth.

"When Jack was about four years old," said he, "he was presented with a hatchet by his generous father", of which, like most boys of his age, he was graciously fond of his new hatchet, and was moving about chopping almost everything that came his way. One day, in the parlour, where he often amused himself hacking away at furniture, he was about to try the edge of his beloved hatchet on one of the legs of his mother's piano. His mother, always alert, espied the approaching attack and immediately flung little Jack against the wall and relieved him of his beloved hatchet. As a result of the hapless conclusion of this event, little Jack never did get the opportunity to state these words to his generous father; "I can't tell a lie, Daddy, - you know I can't tell a lie. I did cut the leg off of Mother's piano with my beloved hatchet."

Another time, ere little Jack was only a babe of two years, his beloved and kind Grandfather, his Mother's Father, was robustly pulling a little red wagon down a hill, with little Jack sitting delightedly within the wagon. Alas, as they were arriving at the bottom of the hill at great speed, the wagon upset and little Jack was hurled to the ground. Undaunted, modest little Jack stood erect, threw back his shoulders, expanded his chest, and proclaimed, "Grandfather, I am not hurt!" He then proceeded to again sit in the little red wagon, and his proud Grandfather resumed his enjoyment in pulling the little red wagon with brave little Jack happily seated within.

One day, little Jack went into the garden and prepared a little bed of finely pulverized earth, then planted some onion sets in neat little rows. His excitement, fanned by expectations of the world's largest onions, was reaching an exuberant pitch as he smoothed the earth over his plantings with his deft little hands. He ran into the house to shout his glee over his accomplishment. The next day, early in the morning, as the birds chirped, and as the sun was slowly sucking the dew into the atmosphere, little Jack approached his onion patch to discover to his dismay that no onions had yet sprouted above the ground. Not to be subdued, and always ready to investigate unresolved problems, little Jack immediately began excavating the onion sets with his little fingers, exposing their rooty bottoms. He then proceeded to examine these bottoms for signs of growth. It was in this way, with his fingers and his head, that he conducted a thorough analysis of the growth situation, the conclusions of which resulted in tender disappointment to the little lad. But, with undaunting confidence in the divine spirit, and in his own ability to grow onions, he proceeded to again backfill the rows of this garden patch. Every few days, he would again investigate the roots of his onion sets to see if they were growing, but to no avail.

Fortunately, little Jack's mind was always cluttered with ideas to follow, and things to do. Therefore, he forgot about his onion patch for several weeks. Then one day, lo and behold, he trudged into the garden, and there before him, standing as straight as her majesty's guards, were row after row of onion stalks. Little Jack proceeded immediately to remove several of the plants from the bed, and sure enough there were onions on them. Jack grabbed a handful, ran into the house to show them to his patient Mother. Then he ran to the neighbour's house to sell the onions to Mrs. Shipe for five cents.

In those days, as many families still do, Easter Sunday was celebrated by the arrival of a large rabbit, commonly known as "The Easter Bunny". This rabbit would leave a basket of candies and elaborately coloured, boiled, chicken eggs for each of the children in the household. At first dawn on Easter morning, little, excited Jack would jump out of bed, run down the steps to the parlour, and search for the basket, which was always slightly hidden. Once finding the basket, he would pull out his chocolate bunnies, bite off their heads, which he ate delightedly, and place the remains of the bunny back in the basket. He would also crack and peel the elaborately coloured, boiled, chicken eggs, eat the whites of the eggs, then roll the yolks under the piano, for he did not particularly care to eat them.

Another event, which occurred during Jack's fourth year in the previously mentioned Mount Union School, was an example of Jack's ready willingness to assist where he deemed it necessary. It seems, one day during his fourth grade class being taught by the stormy Mr. George Vought, Jack had concluded that Mr. Vought's lecture was rather boring. Feeling great sadness for the class in their discomfort and boredom, Jack took it upon himself to liven up the classroom. It seems little Jack was wearing a black bowtie with a stretch neckband. He deftly removed the bowtie, during the boring lecture, and placed it upon his head in the manner of a girl's head bow. In so doing, he looked across the room toward his friend, Harry Harper, and proceeded to make funny faces. Mr. Vought, however, not understanding the true spirit of the event, approached little Jack from behind and swatted him on the rear with the large, wooden paddle that he always carried. Thus the great effort of young Jack was ended, but the classroom was again awake and ready to proceed with their lessons.

One cold, wintry day, when Jack was in the fourth grade, his brother, David, was in the fifth grade. It seems that David was entertaining himself alongside a ramp on the side of the school which led into the furnace room of the school. There was a pipe railing alongside the ramp. David was amusing himself by touching the cold railing with his tongue, then pulling back when the tongue began sticking to the railing. However, he, at one point, curled his tongue way out and around the railing. The tongue immediately froze fast to the ice cold rail. Now young Jack, upon seeing this, advanced to observe very closely to see just what his big brother was doing. David was gurgling something, but Jack, in his scientific, but modest manner, was excited about this great fete of his brother, and thought that it was a great accomplishment, so much so that it did not matter to him what his brother was trying to say. The fact is, Jack was so

188

excited about this great experiment that he did not even realize that his brother's tongue was hopelessly stuck to the rail.

As Jack was observing this experiment of science, other less scientifically minded children saw what was happening and ran into the school and brought out the teacher, Miss Evelyn Brunner, to show her what David was doing. Aghast, she ran into the school and brought out a glass of warm water which she poured gently over David's tongue. This melted the ice and David's tongue was released intact.

As a young lad, Jack immediately showed signs of his great engineering ability. It seems that he and his brothers wanted to build a hut, as most young lads wish to do. In his own invincible way, young Jack always came up with the unusual and original ideas, as he continued to do in his adulthood. At this time, he chose to build his hut underground. He and his brothers dug a large hole, several feet deep, with the hole cut open to the surface of the ground at an adjacent bank. They then proceeded to place wooden timbers, and boards over the top, which was covered with about a foot of earth. The hut was totally concealed, with only the small, tunneled entrance visible.

This hut was regularly used by Jack, his brothers, and their friends as a place of meeting and frivolity. On one occasion, which was around the time of the approaching Halloween season, it seems that the lads chose to throw hog corn, which was readily available in the nearby fields, onto the porches of some nearby houses. This provided charming sounds within the houses, closely resembling the sound of freshly falling rain. It further served to provide food for those who had chickens. The intent was noble. However, one neighbour, one Max Baslick, misconstrued the generosity of the occasion and proceeded to exit his house in a fury to confront the innocent young children. The group of boys immediately ran to their underground hut and entered therein, making great talk of their successful retreat to safety.

Unknown to our young friends, the misguided Mr. Baslick stood outside the hut and waited, having heard the many voices coming from underground. The boys, after a short wait within the hut, began exiting so that they could do the same good for other neighbours. Upon their emergence from the hut, they encountered Mr. Baslick who was still waiting. Our hero, little Jack, happened to be standing in a hole when he emerged, so Mr. Baslick erroneously thought he was a very small lad, and chastised the other boys that "they are setting a bad example for the young lad, because, in his innocence, he probably thought they were throwing rocks at the houses, and he may do the same." Of course, Jack knew they were not throwing rocks, but were performing a very nice act for the enjoyment of the neighbours.

Thus was formed the morality, compassion, curiosity, determination, modesty, and foresight of a little boy whose future became an example for all of those who knew him.

CHAPTER III

"Dear Father, must ye go?
"Yes, my Son, to the service of my country!"

As a child maintains roots to his home, it is difficult for this tie to be broken, and a new home location accepted. This was true of little Jack, who at this time was in his 12th year, who stated his displeasure upon the family's decision to relocate from their beloved home in Sunnyside to a new home in the nearby village of Tharptown; -Tho the new home was into a house which was built by Jack's Mother's Father about forty years earlier.

Gradually, Jack accepted his new surroundings, a new school, and some new friends. But, though he moved, little Jack did not leave his old friends behind. At every chance, he would hike over the top of the mountain, which separated his new home from his old home, enduring whatever hardships he encountered, and without any utterance of complaint, and spend time with his old friends, his best friends.

Young Jack now attended the "Uniontown School" which was located a short distance from his home. The time spent in this school was unspectacular, but provided Jack with additional learning and virtue which was necessary for his divine destiny in life.

When Jack was a mere lad of ten years, he began working in the Shamokin Cemetery, having been hired for the work by Squire Oscar Dockey, of Sunnyside, who was the Superintendent of the Cemetery, and a friend of Little Jack's Father. Young Jack happily performed his work, doing the work of two boys of greater age. Jack pushed lawnmowers, dug graves, cleaned the inside of mausoleums, and watered flowers. He willingly and cheerfully performed any work assigned to him. Jack continued working at the cemetery, and at the Dockey homestead, for years to come. Such work prepared him for the great works of his future life.

In about his twelfth year, Jack was showing signs of his genius. One day, as he tinkered in the workshop in the basement of the McSherry house, which consisted of woodworking machines on a large wooden workbench, such machines having been given to him and his brothers by his generous Uncle Bertlette, the brother of his Mother. Jack proceeded to take an old radio speaker, connected it into the electrical power, and found, much to his delight, that upon holding the two wires which came from the speaker, he would get a jolting electrical shock.

With exuberance, he hailed his older brother, David, to come into the basement from where he was upstairs. David came to the basement, whence Jack told him to hold the two wires, which he did. Then Jack threw the electrical switch, whereby David received a jolting shock, dropped the wires, and proceeded to return upstairs. Then Jack began to connect the wires onto, and among the various pieces of machinery on the workbench. Again, he hailed David to the basement. This time, David, being no fool, stated that he would not hold the wires, and thereupon leaned on the flat area of the circular saw platform. Jack again threw the electrical switch, and once again jolted David. Whereupon, David again proceeded to go upstairs. Then Jack rewired his contraption in another way and again called David downstairs. Jack volunteered to touch the machinery, and asked David to throw the electrical switch. David decided this would be good, and he would enjoy jolting Jack. However, when he threw the switch, which was made of metal, David again was jolted. He proceeded to return upstairs, and stayed there. David, of course, was very proud of his young brother's genius and knew some day he would be honoured by his brother's fame and world reknown.

Scarcely had Jack attained his thirteenth year, before his Father was recalled to service into the United States Navy. As is too often the case, the world was in a turmoil whereby power-hungry, self-serving, greedy political scavengers were trying to oppress the world, and at the same time were murdering innocent people to accomplish their barbaric goals.

Alas, only seven months after Jack's father was recalled into the Navy, the Japanese nation launched a cowardly attack against the United States Naval Base at Pearl Harbor, Hawaii. Thus began a four year world conflict, which plunged the world into an abyss of gloom and darkness, the details of which are too well known in American History, and need not be mentioned here.

Although Jack's father went to sea, and posed a severe threat to the stealthy and murderous submarines of the German Empire, which were operating off the east coast of the United States, he did, on occasion, manage to visit his family at their home in Tharptown. When he arrived home, in his glorious blue uniform, emblazoned with gold insignia, he was held in awe by all those who saw him. Young Jack was greatly impressed by the majestic appearance of his Father. Alas, though, the visits were much too short, and little Jack missed his Father when he was gone again.

During the war, young Jack furthered his learning at a municipal school known as "Coal Township High School" located at Shamokin, Pennsylvania. It is often said, that, among his other studies, Jack studied Latin; but Jack had always maintained that he did not study Latin, although he does agree that he did attend such classes. However, ere the war was over, not only was Jack's Father in the Navy, but Jack's older brothers, William and David were also enlisted into the Naval Service. Finally, on his seventeenth birthday, our hero also joined the Navy and did his part to bring down the surrender of the evil German and Japanese empires.

Finally, the war was over, William and David returned home, but Jack's Father was not relieved of this naval service until over a year after the war had ended. Finally he then returned home. In the meantime, young Jack remained in the naval service of his Country, at his own volition, so that he could accomplish world peace through his great ability to convince man to treat his fellow man with respect and decency. Thus began the adult career of our great hero.

CHAPTER IV

Tis an honourable deed,
tho a dangerous one,
for a brave adventurer
to mediate for peace.

As Jack continued his service in the United States navy, he was assigned to one of the foremost, top of the line, warships of the United States Fleet, the USS Huntington. The ship was in Philadelphia, Pennsylvania at the time Jack went aboard, and still lay an uncommissioned ship, having only recently been launched.

With Jack's assignment to the ship, she was immediately put into commission. At the commissioning ceremonies, as a quartermaster reached for the halyards to raise the flag of the United states to the foremast of the Huntington, at the appropriate time, and for the first time, McSherry exclaimed, "Give me those halyards, for I must be the first to raise the flag of the United States to the foremast of the Huntington, this great ship which will guide the future of the Atlantic Fleet through tumultuous times". Jack thus raised the national flag to the foremast of the great Huntington, for the first time, on this chilly day, the 23rd of February 1946.

Soon after the Huntington was placed into commission, she began her maiden voyage, a "shakedown" cruise to Guantanamo Bay, Cuba. As the new and great ship cruised down the Delaware River, McSherry's steady hand was on the helm, much to the comfort of the entire crew; and after several hours, she gracefully furrowed the waves of the Atlantic with her mighty prow positioned toward Cuba.

The purpose of the shakedown cruise is to confirm that the ship, and her men, will function in the manner planned, and to provide both the ship and the men the opportunity to perform the various intricacies expected of them. The Huntington, and her crew, performed honourably. It is said that this is not always the case. Some ships, on their shakedown cruise, and their crew, may not meet the expectations of those in command. Word has it, that, on the shakedown cruise of the freakish Battle Cruiser, USS Guam, in the midst of the great war, the ship was destined to become helplessly adrift in the Atlantic Ocean, an indefensible target for the ruthless submarines of the German Empire, all because one foolish electricians mate threw the wrong switch. Woe be to the crew that has such a man on their ship.

Gloriously returning to her berth at the Philadelphia Navy Yard, upon completion of the successful and unsurpassed shakedown cruise, the Huntington was met by cheering throngs all along both banks of the Delaware River, and upon mooring at the dock, bands were playing, and people were cheering. Thus is the glory of accomplishing your task with resounding success.

During all of the aforedescribed celebration, the undaunted and modest McSherry was steadfastly steering the ship past the rocks and shoals and other hazards of the Delaware River, and deftly laying her alongside the pier for a perfect landing.

No sooner had the Huntington arrived at the Philadelphia Navy Yard, when President Harry S. Truman directed that the USS Huntington proceed to the free city of Trieste. Mr. Truman knew that the most formidable ship in the United States fleet had on board the wise, honourable, and dauntless, though modest, McSherry. Trieste, located at the northeast border of Italy, and directly adjacent to Jugoslavia, was in the state of anarchy. Mobs from Jugoslavia were confronting mobs of Italians, all in an effort to show the world that each of these unruly mobs was the best qualified to govern Trieste. Mr. Truman wisely chose the USS Huntington, and the great McSherry to proceed to that city to quell the riots, becalm the people, and restore order and happiness.

During the crossing of the Atlantic, when McSherry was carrying out his duties in the pilot house, it was brought to his attention that, one, William Scharninghausen, had been sent to the pilot house by his division officer to steer the ship. Scharninghausen stated that there must have been some mistake, as he had never steered a ship before, and didn't even know how to steer a ship. Furthermore, he stated, as a civilian, before entering the navy, he couldn't even drive a car.

Pondering this situation, McSherry concluded that he would allow Scharninghausen to steer the ship. McSherry was impressed by the man's honesty in stating that he could not steer a ship, nor even a car. Since the Atlantic was very large, and there were not many ships on it at the time, Scharninghausen was allowed to take over the helm, but under the very watchful and jaundiced eye of McSherry. Fortunately, Scharninghausen hit nothing during his four-hour watch, and managed to stay within ten degrees of the designated course, therefore, he became a certified helmsman and performed his duties well thereafter.

Upon arriving in Trieste, McSherry began the difficult task assigned by the President. McSherry made many trips to the mainland, and throughout the city. He discussed peace and mutual respect to any Italian or Jugoslav, which he encountered, whom could understand English.

On one occasion, McSherry chose to travel overland from Trieste, through the forests and fields, and across very dangerous mine fields to approach the Jugoslav people, in their own land, thereby delivering, personally, President Truman's message for peace. Many years after the occurrence of this brave event, a Jugoslav farmer, who happened to be present at the time the dauntless, extremely brave, but modest, McSherry boldly strode across the minefield, came forward and stated the following. "As I saw this physically grand person approach the minefield, I was dismayed to think how he would be blown into oblivion, then I recognized him as the noble and fearless McSherry, and watched in awe as he walked across those mines, totally protected by the almighty. The almighty had greater things planned for McSherry. He could not be destroyed by a minefield".

While at Trieste, the Huntington was ordered to go to Venice, Italy, which was nearby, a mere nine hours cruise from Trieste. The purpose of this voyage was to investigate the political atmosphere of the City, and at the same time, determine whether the City was actually sinking into the sea. However, upon arriving in Venice, Lieutenant Privy was sent ashore to make a preliminary appraisal of the situation. Upon observing that all of the streets were flooded, for Privy did not know that the City was built in the water and contained canals, he ran throughout the City shouting "Run for the hills! The dam is broken!" On and on he ran, throughout the entire city, frightening the citizens, and causing wild chaos as the people were running around, shouting, "Where is the high ground! Where is the high ground". Upon noticing this, Privy-induced panic, McSherry immediately left the ship and soothed the populace. Privy was sent back to the ship, put before Commander Gregor at Captain's Mast, and was sent to the ship's brig.

Thereupon, McSherry observed the glorious buildings, bridges and canals within the City by walking the narrow, moss-covered, walkways along the canals, and by cruising the canals in a long, black gondola which was being poled along by a cheerful Venetian singing "O Solo Mio". After much observation, it was McSherry's conclusion that the City was not sinking into the Ocean, but, in fact, the Ocean was rising into the City. He was positive of this when he noted the gondolas, which were tied to poles in the canals, rising gradually over an extended time. He thus made the appropriate report to the Authorities.

In September 1946, the Huntington arrived in Naples, Italy, which was located near the Ruins of Pompeii. Pompeii had been totally covered with ashes from the eruption of Mount Vesuvius about 2000 years earlier. Since that time, archeologists have uncovered much of the City. McSherry, and several aides, chose to adventure to Pompeii to make a first hand investigation of the City as only the great McSherry would be wont to do. There was much evidence there to indicate that the civilization that once lived there was lacking in morals, and promoted a very decadent society. This was not necessarily a new revelation, because Historians have been concluding on that for quite some time. However, McSherry noticed, also, that there were very deep ruts, from the cart and chariot wheels, in all of the stone streets. Knowing that the citizens were heavily taxed, he wondered why these streets were not properly repaired and maintained. Further investigation disclosed that the politicians, mostly lawyers, were corrupt, and used the street maintenance funds for their entertainment and vices. McSherry sent his report to the Government of Italy for their information and file.

As time passed, the USS Huntington, with McSherry aboard, was ordered to proceed to Alexandria, Egypt, for the sole purpose of displaying the American flag and guaranteeing all peoples that they would be protected from any evil, no matter what it may be. Early upon his arrival in Alexandria, McSherry was walking from the ship into the downtown area of Alexandria. He was prior informed that the area through which he was walking was heavily populated by vandals, assassins, robbers, and all forms of evil persons who would set upon the helpless as they naively walked through the area. This did not concern the dauntless and brave, but modest McSherry. Indeed, he was set upon by hordes of vandals, assassins and robbers who threatened him and foolishly tried to rob him. McSherry stood his ground and merely stared at them very coldly. Someone among the vandals recognized McSherry and shouted out, "That fearless man is the great McSherry, don't attempt to attack him. Run away! Run away"! With that, the hordes of vandals, assassins, robbers and evil persons ran in all directions, and the streets were immediately cleared. McSherry then continued his walk to the downtown area.

In November 1946, McSherry departed from Alexandria for his world famous excursion to the Pyramids and sphinx of Gizeh. It was not commonly known at the time, but McSherry was sent to observe these antiquities because of his Engineering genius. It was not until many years later that it was disclosed that McSherry consulted with the Government of Egypt to recommend ways to eliminate the on-going erosion of the foundations, especially of the Sphinx; And to further find a way to reinforce the support of the head of the Sphinx so that it would not eventually shear off and fall to the ground, totally destroyed! McSherry made such recommendations, and they were successfully carried out.

The expedition to the Pyramids and Sphinx was a major undertaking. The first leg of the trip was made by train, along the Nile, from Alexandria to Cairo. At that point, McSherry transferred to a bus, much in need of repairs, but which managed to trudge the sandy roads of the desert, through herds of camels, and among the wild-eyed water buffalo. Finally he reached the pyramids. Upon reaching his destination, he scanned the many Arabs present, and asked who would provide him with torchlight for his entry into the darkness of the passages and tombs of the great pyramid. The Arabs, knowing who he was, all shouted to be the honoured one to carry the torches. Rioting broke out as each Arab wanted to be the chosen one. In his calming way, McSherry stopped the rioting, and chose two bearded old men to carry the torches for him.

McSherry, with the flickering light of the two torches carried by the chosen and honoured Arabs, made his way into the dismal passageways, as the light of the torches transmitted flickering shadows on the walls, up the winding, and very narrow, stone stairways. In all of his modesty, he even crawled on his hands and knees to enter the great tomb room of Cheops. Spending several hours within the dimness of the pyramid, he recorded all of the structural features, and the total layout of the pyramid into his unparalleled memory.

Upon emerging from the pyramid, amidst the cheers of thousands of Arabs, McSherry proceeded to acquire a camel, a snorting, ferocious beast, which he calmly and professionally mounted, then persuaded to move into the desert and toward the Sphinx. Totally in control of this obnoxious beast, he arrived safely at the Sphinx, whereupon he immediately examined and memorized all of the intricate details of the construction of this monument. He was, thus, prepared to meet with the Egyptian officials to make his recommendations for repair and preservation. The route back to Alexandria was the reverse of the process in which he arrived at Gizeh. Having thus saved these fabulous antiquities, he returned to his duty on the USS Huntington at Alexandria.

Some time thereafter, the Huntington was ordered to Livorno, sometimes called Leghorn, Italy. This town, having been totally destroyed by the presence of World War II, was located near to the Leaning Tower of Pisa. It was deemed appropriate that the genius of McSherry should be made available to the Italian Government to determine why the tower was leaning, whose fault it was, and what to do to correct it.

In order to make the trip to Pisa, the ship approached the harbour of Livorno. The harbour was cluttered with sunken ships, their hulls and masts partially above water. Those responsible for directing the ship into the harbour said it could not be done. The Huntington was eighty feet wide at the beam, and the widest opening between the sunken ships was only eighty-seven feet, hardly enough clearance through which to pass an unwieldy ship. McSherry, in all of his calmness, stated, "I can steer the Huntington through that opening, after all, she is the sleekest ship in the United States Fleet." With this, McSherry took the helm and steered the ship unwaveringly through the narrow opening. Upon this accomplishment, the ship's crew, along with the hordes on the shore, took up an incessant cheering which went on for hours.

Whereupon, the ship was moored to the dock, and the gangplank lowered, McSherry, with his aide, Herbert Miller, took off for Pisa. The journey was difficult, since they had no means of transportation of their own, relying totally on the method of travel commonly known as hitchhiking. After some close encounters along the way, they made the journey safely to Pisa.

Upon locating the tower, McSherry and Miller proceeded to climb to the top. McSherry noted that it was at this point where Galileo had dropped a brick and a half to the ground below. He deemed that the blame for the leaning of the Tower could very well rest with Galileo, since the impact of the bricks hitting the ground could have vibrated the sands in the foundation bed, creating the settlement and resultant leaning of the Tower. McSherry forwarded his report and opinions to the office of the Bureau of Antiquities in Rome. To this day, the exact contents of the report are not known to those outside the Italian government, however, it is believed that some day the repairs and restoration procedures recommended by McSherry will be carried out.

Other areas visited by the USS Huntington were Oran, Algeria;

Malta; Genoa, Italy; the free city of Tangier; Rapallo, Italy; Taranto, Italy; Villefranche and Nice, France; Marseilles, France; Maddalena Island; and Gibraltar. It was then determined that McSherry was needed back in the United States to be dispatched to other areas of the world that desperately needed his genius and foresight to solve indeterminate problems. With that, the ship made a daring crossing over the Atlantic during a violent storm, which caused waves in excess of forty feet in height, along with high winds. The Huntington rolled as much as thirty nine degrees off the vertical during this storm. Of course, the helm and the compass of the ship were under the watchful eye of McSherry, who seldom left the pilot house.

Upon arrival in Narragansett Bay, at Newport, Rhode Island, McSherry was transferred from the Huntington to several destroyers, on which he served for a short time. It seems that these ships were towing targets for the larger ships of the fleet to practice firing their large guns. Scrutinizing the situation, and realizing the extreme danger to the crews of the destroyers engaged in such hazardous duty, McSherry developed a system whereby, instead of firing at targets towed by the destroyers, the gunners on the larger ships would be sent, in relays, to Coney Island, New York, where they could practice shooting in the arcades. Having made this ingenious recommendation, McSherry was then sent to Panama where his headquarters would be aboard the USS Orion, a submarine tender.

CHAPTER V

God made two oceans,
Separated by thirty miles of land,
Teddy Roosevelt joined them,
By cutting through the land.

Because it was commonly believed that the surface elevation of the Pacific Ocean was lower than the surface of the Atlantic Ocean, there was concern among the owners of the shipping fleets of the Atlantic, that the construction of the canal across the Isthmus of Panama was going to, over time, siphon the water from the Atlantic into the Pacific, thereby lowering the water level in the Atlantic so ports would become too shallow for the passage of the ships. Furthermore, the ports would end up high on a hill above the new water level.

To allay these fears, McSherry cruised through the Panama Canal four times at the helm of the USS Orion. Each time, he studied the excavations of the canal, as well as the rise and fall at each of the locks, including the Gatun Lake locks, the Miraflores locks, and the Pedro Miguel locks. His observations and measurements were such that he had determined that the Atlantic Ocean and the Pacific Ocean each had the same surface elevation, and siphonage of water through the canal would not occur. This conclusion was welcome news to all of the shippers of the Atlantic, and to the people along the East Coast of the United States. It is interesting to note that the main excavation in the canal occurred at what was originally known as the Culebra Cut, however, the name of this excavation was changed to the Gaillard Cut in honor of the Engineer in charge of the work. Today, in the shipping and engineering circles, this cut is widely known as the McSherry Cut.

Another problem that existed in Panama was the fact that the Old City of Panama was burned to the ground in the 1600's. McSherry, on the back of a wild, fiery, native horse, rode to the site of the old City. He noted that most of the buildings were totally destroyed, except a bell tower which was constructed of stone. Another building that partially survived was a convent that was also constructed of stone. Taking into consideration all of these facts, McSherry, in all of his wisdom, had determined that the City had apparently existed without a building code, which surely would have contained the necessary requirements to prevent such extensive fire-related damage. As a result, thereof, he recommended to the Panamanian government that they enact a strict building code, which would include unreasonable requirements for the protection of the buildings against fire damage, to the extent that it is impossible to burn any building even if attacked by plundering pirates. Or, as an alternate idea, McSherry suggested that the government of Panama could pass an ordinance which would make it unlawful for pirates to possess matches. The Panamanian Government thanked President Truman for sending McSherry to Panama to solve these serious problems.

CHAPTER VI

To learn creates knowledge
Knowledge creates better income
Hence, it's time for College
With the right curriculum.

Having returned, in 1949, to his native country, McSherry, over protests of President and Mrs. Truman, and the officialdom of the United States Navy, chose to resign from the Naval Service to attend to other matters of great importance. First, he returned to his native Pennsylvania to consult with his wise Father and his patient Mother. While remaining at his home for a brief period of time, he once again was employed by Squire Dockey to oversee the maintenance of his vast plantation in the village of Sunnyside. Squire Dockey's wife, Marian, scheduled the work to be accomplished on the plantation. This brings us to the point that a person should never discount the knowledge of others, because everyone knows something that others do not know. This is illustrated in fact by the following episode on the plantation. Lady Dockey had determined that the maintenance people should plant hundreds of small pine trees on the property. McSherry stated that he was ready to proceed with the project immediately. To this, Lady Dockey retorted, "No! No!, we must not plant the trees until ascension day, then they will grow into healthy trees without fail". McSherry was taken aback by this statement of scientific brilliance, and waited about a week until ascension day to plant the trees. Just as Lady Dockey stated, the trees grew in a healthy manner to great heights.

Another similar display of scientific brilliance by Lady Dockey was the event about to be described. One beautiful, sunny morning, McSherry was preparing to begin his duties on the plantation when Lady Dockey noticed that he had several warts on the fingers of his left hand, something that he had not previously possessed. She immediately began prescribing several different procedures whereby the warts can be removed. One method was to take a slice of a potato which contained an eye, which is a sprout on the surface of the potato, and spread from the potato slice the juice onto the warts, then plant the potato slice in the field. As the new potato plant grows, the warts will disappear. An alternate method which she prescribed was to get a wooden shingle from a house or barn, cut a v-notch into the end of the shingle, then throw it over your left shoulder and never look at it again. The warts will, thence, immediately disappear. Her brilliance in such things was never matched. After several days, McSherry arrived at work with no warts on his fingers. Lady Dockey excitedly asked what he had done to get rid of the warts. McSherry responded with honesty and appreciation that the evening prior he had cut a notch into a wooden shingle and threw it over his left shoulder never to look at it again. Lady Dockey was pleased.

As McSherry worked on the plantation, in the hot sun, doing the work of several people, he sometimes developed a thirst, but in all of his self-control and manliness, he never asked lady Dockey for a drink. She, of course, in her consideration and kindness would occasionally offer McSherry a drink of water. But, in her wisdom and great knowledge of such things, she would give McSherry only a very small glass of water, because too much would not be good for him in the heat, and the water was at room temperature because cold water would not be good for him. In addition, the water contained several drops of orange juice to abate any other ill effects. This caution and gentle care was greatly appreciated by McSherry.

After spending the summer with his parents and working for Squire Dockey, when the autumn leaves began to colour, McSherry left home to attend college at the institution of higher learning known as Indiana Technical College in Fort Wayne, Indiana. Even though it would conceivably be the most difficult curriculum in the college for most people, McSherry chose to study Civil Engineering. With his genius, he progressed well, and, in what seemed like a very short time, in the year 1952 he graduated with honors with the degree, Bachelor of Science in Civil Engineering.

Upon graduation from college, McSherry returned to Pennsylvania where he discovered that his parents had moved to the Borough of Camp Hill in his absence. He temporarily lived in their home as he sought employment in the local area. At the first business whereby he ventured for the possibility of employment, he entered the front door of the establishment where he came to two stairways, one went up and one went down. Hearing voices in each direction, he chose to go up the steps. At the top of the steps there was an old, white-haired gentlemen sitting behind a desk in his office. McSherry walked in, introduced himself and said he was looking for employment as a Civil Engineer. The gentleman, Mr. Charles C. Conrad, who happened to be the head of the Dams and Waterworks Division of the company, known as Gannett, Fleming, Corddry, and Carpenter, Inc., immediately hired McSherry without even asking for any particular qualifications because he had heard of the many accomplishments of McSherry throughout the world. Thus McSherry became a dam engineer.

THE END

Made in the USA
Middletown, DE
19 January 2020